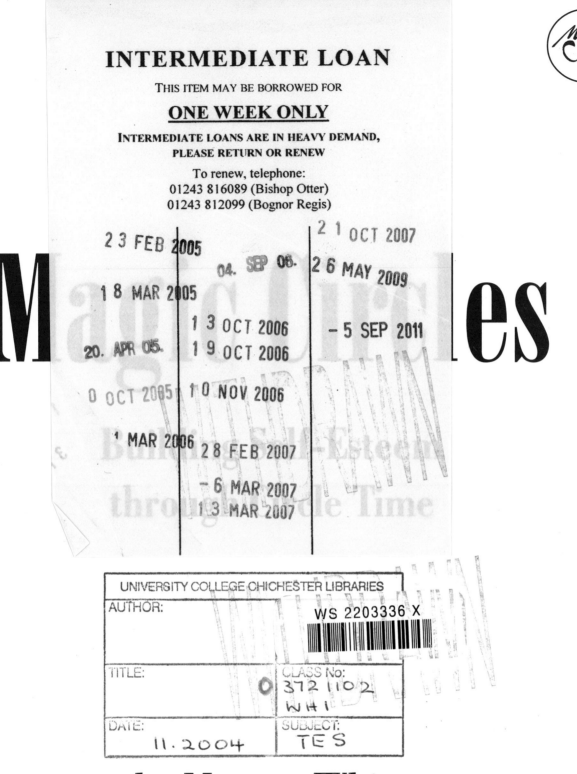

INTERMEDIATE LOAN

THIS ITEM MAY BE BORROWED FOR

ONE WEEK ONLY

INTERMEDIATE LOANS ARE IN HEAVY DEMAND,
PLEASE RETURN OR RENEW

To renew, telephone:
01243 816089 (Bishop Otter)
01243 812099 (Bognor Regis)

23 FEB 2005

2 1 OCT 2007

04. SEP 06. 2 6 MAY 2009

18 MAR 2005

1 3 OCT 2006 − 5 SEP 2011

20. APR 05. 1 9 OCT 2006

0 OCT 2005 1 0 NOV 2006

1 MAR 2006 28 FEB 2007

− 6 MAR 2007
1 3 MAR 2007

Magic Circles

Building Self-Esteem through Circle Time

by Murray White

previously published by Daniels Publishing as
Self-Esteem : Its meaning and value in schools A & B

Lucky Duck Publishing
3, Thorndale Mews, Clifton,
Bristol BS8 2HX

Phone 0117 973 2881 Fax 0117 973 1707
e-mail publishing@luckyduck.co.uk
website www.luckyduck.co.uk

ISBN 1 873942 57 5

1

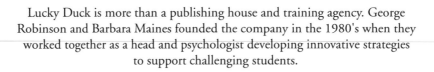

Lucky Duck is more than a publishing house and training agency. George Robinson and Barbara Maines founded the company in the 1980's when they worked together as a head and psychologist developing innovative strategies to support challenging students.

They have an international reputation for their work on bullying, self-esteem, emotional literacy and many other subjects of interest to the world of education.

George and Barbara have set up a regular news-spot on the website. Twice yearly these items will be printed as a newsletter. If you would like to go on the mailing list to receive this then please contact us:

Lucky Duck Publishing Ltd. 3 Thorndale Mews, Clifton, Bristol, BS8 2HX, UK

Phone: 0044 (0)117 973 2881   e-mail newsletter@luckyduck.co.uk
Fax: 044 (0)117 973 1707   website www.luckyduck.co.uk

ISBN: 1 873 942 57 5

Lucky Duck Publishing Ltd
3 Thorndale Mews, Clifton, Bristol, BS8 2HX

www.luckyduck.co.uk

Printed by Antony Rowe Limited

Foreword

When we started Lame Duck Publishing (now Lucky Duck) in 1988 it was a vehicle for our first publication on self esteem. About the same time we heard of a head teacher in Cambridge-shire who was doing exciting work with children raising their self esteem using a technique he called magic circles. We followed his progress seeing the positive press he received in The Times Educational Supplement. In 1991 he published the first comprehensive U.K. book on Circle Time.

We were thrilled, two years later, to meet this influential person, who has done so much to promote the use of Circle Time in British schools. We were honoured when, in 1998, he approached us to publish his books and to promote his work.

Thank you Murray, your faith in Lucky Duck has boosted our self esteem.

This publication is a revised version of,

> White, Murray. (1991). Self Esteem. Its meaning and value in schools.
> Set A and Set B. Published by Daniels.

It has been updated and edited to combine both sets into one volume.

The basic requirement is not talent but purpose. The human race is competitive and success comes from the pursuit of individual excellence. Your real competitor is not the body of men and women with whom you work - your real competitor is you. So compete continually with yourself to improve your performance. Do what you can, with that you have, where you are. Don't dilute your effort with many different objectives; decide the most important thing to do at any time and do it well. Don't just conform; dare to be different. Use your imagination, not only to foresee the future but also to make it possible. And remember that success is a journey, not a destination.

Sir Arthur Sugden, Chief Executive, Co-operative Wholesale Society

Magic Circles

Acknowledgements

The author is grateful to:

The children of Braybrook Primary School, Peterborough for sharing Circle Times.

Kenneth Tutt, head teacher of Braybrook Primary School, and the staff, for their support and co-operation.

Joan Stark, Ormsgill Infant School, Cumbria, for her study of the introduction of Circle Time in her school.

Jonathan Darrell and his class at Kings' Hedges Junior School, Cambridge for a summary of their discussion on behaviour.

The many teachers who have sent me their observations about the benefits of Circle Time to the children in their classes.

John Heron, author of Helping the Client etc. for the 'diagrams of behaviour change' principle on page 21.

B Remsberg and A Saunders, authors of Help Your Child Cope with Stress, Piatkus Books, for the Quick Relax.

Please note that "he" and "she" are interchangeable.

Contents

"Probably the most important requirement for effective behaviour, central to the whole problem, is self-esteem."

Stanley Coopersmith: The Antecedents of Self-Esteem

Introduction

Every teacher wishes for a class of pupils who all take pleasure in behaving well and are all keen to study. A room which contains such a class is a good place to be, an ideal learning environment. In order to achieve such a situation, the issue of self-esteem must be addressed as self-esteem is the pivotal point between success and failure in school.

It has a marked effect on both behaviour and learning. The connection between behaviour and self-esteem is well documented; behavioural difficulties do not occur where a healthy level of self-esteem is present and research shows that the correlation between self-esteem and school achievement is as high as between IQ and school achievement. Where teachers are aware of, and adopt strategies, which enhance the self-esteem of their pupils, they find that attendance is high, that there is a real enthusiasm to learn and that relationships flourish.

This book is a contribution to the understanding of self-esteem and sets out to show teachers and others responsible for the welfare of children and young people how they can help to enhance their self-esteem, while at the same time developing an awareness of their own. The ideas and strategies presented here are based on my experiences with children and on discussions with teachers and others in staffrooms and workshops over many years. I take this opportunity to express my appreciation to the many super young people and their mentors who shared such a lot of their lives with me.

Circle Times are now being conducted in schools and other settings all over the country for children of all ages. The teachers and leaders concerned need everyone's encouragement and thanks for the vital role they are taking in helping our children and young people attain the self-esteem they need to fulfil their potential and to lead productive, fulfilled lives.

Using this book.

Group leaders are recommended to conduct the Circle Times in the sequence they are presented. They are based on the five building blocks of self-esteem which must be dealt with in the correct order if the raising of self-esteem is to be achieved. Each one of the Circle Times described contains a lot of material and could be done over several sessions. Many of the activities will gain from lots of repetition. In the discussion groups it is important that all those who wish to contribute should be encouraged to do so.

Learning new behaviours or replacing old ones e.g. the shy child gaining confidence to speak to a group or the aggressive one becoming aware of different ways to relate, can take time so persistence is required when embarking on Circle Times. There are, however, often very early clues that the participants are benefiting from the experience and anecdotes abound of the one child in the first or second session who says or does something so dramatic that the teacher can immediately see the value of the process and is inspired to carry on. One example concerns the six year old who had never spoken to anyone other than the teacher since starting school and then felt safe enough to join in a triad and happily tell them about what she had been doing the previous day.

The leader should always to be ready to initiate talk about carrying these different ways and ideas outside the circle into all the other school and home situations and be alert to the chance to encourage and support if present on these occasions. If the teacher is with the group throughout the rest of the day many opportunities will undoubtedly present themselves where the children can use their new learning which they discovered in a Circle Time workshop. Just as a laboratory is a place where experiments are tried so Circle Times are places where new or different ways of being are tried and tested, without fear of failure or ridicule.

If the children can be seen to be enjoying the activities you can be sure that something positive is happening. It is important to give them lots of opportunities to reflect on the process in ways appropriate to their ages. When they begin to appreciate how relevant and worthwhile the ideas put forward in Circle Times are to their daily lives then a solid foundation for high self-esteem will have been laid.

The visualisations -'The Quick Relax ' 'Going On A Trip ' and Discovering Our Inner Strength' found in the section of activities to promote a sense of well-being are included on the audio tape "Picture This : Guided Imagery for Circle Time" also available from Lucky Duck. The booklet which accompanies the tape explains the objective of each of the exercises and explains the value of this activity in raising self-esteem.

These Circle Times were first devised for use with youngsters in the 5 - 14 age range, but much of the material has since been used successfully with older teenagers and adult groups. Imaginative leaders will adapt the activities to suit the circumstances.

Where children are referred to in the text please substitute young people or whatever is appropriate in your situation. Similarly with he and she. Both are used in the text.

For you to do

Emphasis must be put upon the importance of the adults conducting the groups to disclose their own experiences during Circle Times. Young people will share more easily if the leaders act as a model. Consequently the intention of the paragraphs marked 'For You To Do' is to help the teacher or leader to focus on their own level of self-esteem, to understand some of the processes which help to enhance it, and to increase their appreciation of the levels of esteem of others. If adults want to help children and young people develop self-esteem it is essential that they are aware of their own level of self-esteem.

A Sense of Esteem

Teachers affect eternity; no one can tell where their influence stops.

- Source unknown

Children's self-esteem

Self-esteem can be learnt, but it cannot be taught. If we wish to raise a child's self-esteem, our job is to create an environment, and provide experiences, which will help the child discover how to learn it for himself. It is like showing a child how to ride a bicycle. You can demonstrate it yourself and then you can hold him upright in the saddle and run along behind, but the reality is that having made the right safe conditions, you have just got to be there with him while he tries for himself.

> *I regard self-esteem as the single most powerful force in our existence . . . . . the way we feel about ourselves affects virtually every aspect of our existence - work, love, sex, interpersonal relationships of every kind.*
>
> *Nathaniel Branden: The Psychology of Self-Esteem*

To help children grow into mature autonomous adults, a programme and structure designed to promote self-esteem is a first class investment in every school. Often the all important area of emotional development is badly neglected in schools just as the honest expression of feelings seems to be taboo in our culture. It is affective education which gives children the ability to think positively about themselves, to be responsible for themselves, and to make wise decisions. For maximum effect, both cognitive and affective education are needed. Exclusive attention to cognitive skills leaves much of value out of the educative process; such a single focus may result in poor cognitive education. The failure to form a union between emotion and intellect invariably results in wasted effort. The way to raise a child's self-esteem and release potential is through affective education. With today's emphasis on increasing academic performance and excellence it is more important than ever.

> *A person's judgement of self, influences the kinds of friends he chooses, how he gets along with others, the kind of person he marries, and how productive he will be. It affects his creativity, integrity, stability and even whether he will be a leader or a follower. His feelings of self-worth form the core of his personality and determines the use he makes of his aptitudes and abilities. His attitude towards himself has a direct bearing on how he lives all parts of his life. In fact, self-esteem is the mainspring that slates each of us for success or failure as a human being.*
> *Dorothy Corkille Briggs: Your Child's Self-Esteem (Doubleday 1970)*

> *The development of the ability to relate well to pupils should be a key consideration in assessing a student's overall competence to teach.*
> *Recommendation 4.5 from the Report of the Committee of Inquiry into Discipline in Schools, chaired by Lord Elton 1989*

Your self-esteem

The pressures of the educational system today certainly contribute to lack of self-esteem - readers of Ted Wragg's articles in the Times Educational Supplement will be aware of this. Teachers who adopt an authoritarian role or demand strict rules, or constantly criticise and judge, probably lack self-esteem. It is not only the children who will benefit from improved self-esteem, but also the teachers. When negative influences and practices have been detected and replaced by positive attitudes and behaviours, an atmosphere of trust and acceptance is created. In this atmosphere, people's feelings of self-worth are encouraged and teachers are keen to work together.

> *Children don't care how much you know until they know how much you care.*
>
> *Anon*

No matter how knowledgeable and conscientious they are in other areas, teachers need relationship skills; these come with the awareness generated by good self-esteem. A teacher with high self-esteem will enable a child to grow so that he will feel confident to explore new dimensions, set his own goals and become more independent. A teacher with high self-esteem is more willing and able to encourage children having any kinds of difficulties.

> *A child will benefit quite remarkably by modelling his behaviour on an effective, assured and competent individual.*
>
> **Stanley Coopersmith: The Antecedents of Self-Esteem**

For you to do

Before beginning the Circle Time sessions with the children I suggest that you read all of the material, and undertake the personal work, this will help to explain the basic process of enhancing self-esteem.

1. Focus on the last three times you spoke to a child. Was there anything said or done which would have raised her self-esteem?
2. On your next teaching day, identify the negative and positive comments you hear others make. Which of the two categories do you hear most?
3. Make a mental note of the negative and positive comments you hear yourself make. Which of the two categories do you make most?

> *Self-esteem: Appreciating my own worth and importance, and having the character to be accountable for myself and to act responsibly towards others.*
>
> **California Task Force to Promote Self-Esteem and Personal and Social Responsibility**

For you to do

1. What is self-esteem? Either alone, or after discussion with colleagues, decide on a definition.
2. Your own self-esteem. On a continuum of zero to ten, where would you put your self-esteem at this moment?

3. In what circumstances do you find your self-esteem low? In what situations do you find your self-esteem high? What makes the difference?

At its best, teaching, like life, is a process of learning more about ourselves and sharing that expanded wholeness with students so that they may become more unified. It is a process of finding out who we really are so that we can grant the space to others to find themselves.

G. Hendricks: The Centred Teacher

In contemporary society low self-esteem should be considered an enormous public health problem. Patients who report low self-esteem usually say it has been present since early childhood, or at the latest, adolescence . . . The rescue of a substantial proportion of the population from the misery of lifelong low esteem remains a challenge for both educationalists and mental health workers.

The Lancet, 22 October 1988

For you to do

The Johari Window

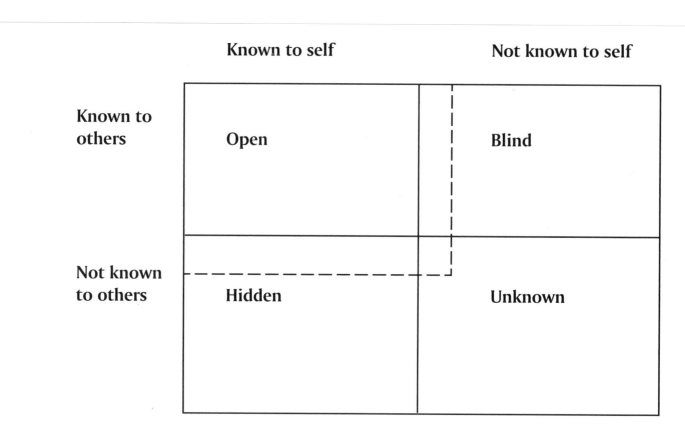

Please look at this diagram (supposedly devised by two friends called John and Harry, hence Johari).

 ♦ Self-disclosure opens the hidden area
 ♦ Feedback opens the blind area
 ♦ Experiment and play open the unknown area

1. Take time to list some circumstances and situations where you have opened your window, however slightly.

2. Self-esteem is based on openness and trust. Where have you been and who have you been with when you have:

 disclosed things to others which weren't known before?

 had information from others about how your behaviour appears to them?

 discovered something new about yourself?

 What amount of risk do you think you took?

 Was there more trust between you and the others afterwards?

 Did your feelings towards yourself change in any way?

3. Discuss the answers with a friend.

Circle Time helps children to open their windows and to set their sights on new horizons.

The importance of self-esteem in schools

The problem with life is that the good bits last about five seconds flat and the bad bits five million hours.
Alexander, an eight year old, speaking on the television programme "Citizen 2000"
25 February 1991

I believe children are born with total esteem. However, early in life many have experiences and encounter situations which quickly lead them to form beliefs and behave in ways which hinder their true growth, limit their potential and unless changed will forever prevent them from becoming mature autonomous people - what Carl Rogers calls "fully functioning" - and not allow them to have happy and successful lives. As these restrictive beliefs and behaviour problems become established so does a poor opinion of themselves and the result is low self-esteem.

The good news is that this never need be a permanent state. Self-esteem can always be changed and enhanced. This possibility is open to all regardless of background, gender, race, or any other category. There is no mystery about it; new personal skills and a change of attitude is all that is required. We can aim to develop and nourish our self-esteem at any age, and, as adults, we owe it to ourselves to do that. Also, as adults, if we have responsibility for the welfare and education of children then we owe it to them to provide every opportunity to develop their self-esteem.

For you to do

Success is only temporary, delaying failure.

Graham Greene

Every day is a new opportunity, every crisis a new challenge.

John Heron

♦ Examine your feelings when considering these statements.
♦ Which one feels more comfortable?
♦ Can you identify any recurring thoughts which you have and which give the same message as the one you have chosen?

Students who feel good about themselves and their abilities are the ones most likely to succeed.
W. Purkey, School Concept and School Achievement

If we can help children develop self-esteem we are not only improving their chances for a successful school career but for a successful life as well. While we are dealing with their present we are investing for their future, as well as in the benefits to society. HM Inspectors certainly believe in the value of this work.

Personal and Social Education is concerned with qualities and attitudes, knowledge and understanding, and abilities and skills in relation to oneself and others, social responsibilities and morality. It helps pupils be considerate and enterprising in the present, while it prepares them for an informed and active involvement in family, social, economic and civil life.

Curriculum Matter 14, 1989, PSE from 5 to 16

A study conducted by the National Institute of Education in America asked 1000 people aged 30 if they felt their education had equipped them with "the skills needed in the real world." More than 80% said absolutely not and when asked what skills they wish they had been taught, put at the top of the list relationship skills ("how do I get along better with the people I'm living with?").

I don't think this opinion is confined to those in the United States. Politicians in this country who are seeking answers to cope with the increasing problems caused by violence and crime among our youth would do well to consider how the composition of the National Curriculum squeezes PSE into a very tight corner of the timetable. They should understand, as teachers do, that if we give more time to PSE, or, as I prefer to call it, affective education, then we are giving children the skills which have to be the priorities in everyone's life.

For you to do

Which would you prefer to know?
- ♦ How to relate well to partners, friends, employers, employees?
- ♦ The names and dates of the kings and queens of England?
- ♦ Pythagoras' theorem?
- ♦ How to bring up thriving children?

In any case, there is no real conflict. It does not have to be an either/or situation. What is needed, as I've said before and want to emphasize strongly, is a better balance between cognitive and affective education. If we bring that about then levels of achievement in mathematics, science, language, etc., will rise, as Purkey suggests, in spite of the apparent paradox that less time is being spent on academic subjects.

Rudimentary guidance to the promotion of self-esteem already exists in the National Curriculum. It states that at:

Key Stage One

Children should: understand the importance of valuing oneself and others; begin to understand the range of human emotions and ways to deal with these; begin to be able to co-operate with others in work and play.

Key Stage Two

Children should: recognise that individuals belong to many groups in which they will have different roles; understand that individual responses to events will vary and respect other people's emotions and feelings; understand that actions have consequences for oneself and others; understand the meaning of friendship and loyalty and begin to develop skills needed to form relationships.

Key Stage Three

Children should: know how labelling and stereotyping can have a negative effect on mental health; be able to give and receive praise and encouragement in order to promote the self-esteem and self-confidence essential to mental health; understand the emotional changes which take place during puberty; understand differences in maturation and have a positive self-image.

Key Stage Four

Children should: be able to carry out honest self-assessment; appreciate ways in which they can control aspects of their own behaviour and resist peer pressure; be able to understand and manage changes in relationships; know about factors which influence the process of making decisions, including choosing between alternatives and considering long and short-term consequences of decisions for oneself and others; recognise the causes and effects of stress; be able to identify ways of reducing/managing/preventing stress; know how to ask for and give support; be aware of personal beliefs and prejudices about mental illness.

In my opinion it is wrong to wait until Key Stages Three and Four before working on most of the issues listed there. Children need these skills as early as possible and are perfectly capable of learning and absorbing them when young. The activities in these packs set out to prove just that. I would especially urge readers not to wait until Key Stage Four before dealing with the management of stress. More children than ever are coping with the effects of divorce, unemployment, homelessness, abuse, bullying and need help and support in school. See Stress in Children page 27.

For children in an unrewarding environment, good experiences at school can make quite a big difference . . . (schools) can offer experiences which help certain children and are potentially beneficial to all.

**Michael Rutter, Professor of Child Psychiatry, University of London, quoted in the TES,
March 1990**

I think we owe it to Alexander and his peers to help them make the "good bits" last a bit longer. This definition gives a clear idea of what our aims for them should be:

Self-esteem is a relaxed appreciation of the full extent of one's personality - quirks and all - created by a sum of parts: flexibility, courage, creativity, self-acceptance, self-confidence and a positive self-image. Self-esteem enhances your performance, increases the likelihood of your success, is the jet fuel of motivation, and the bedrock of well being and contentment.

Self magazine, 1990

The teacher's role

Above all, watch with glittering eyes, the whole world around you - because the greatest secrets are always hidden in the most unlikely places. Those who don't believe in magic will never find it.

Roald Dahl, The Minpins - the final words of his last book written for children

Circle Time is like the scaffolding which is erected to support a building while it is being built, it supports the children while they grow and develop their esteem. The teacher is the architect who plans and devises the activities and uses all her skill and experience to give information and assurance at the level the children need. If your intention is to allow the children to grow by experiencing the five stages necessary for self-esteem then you will gently and firmly give them the power to take risks, consider options, make choices and decisions, all in the safe environment of Circle Time.

The teacher as a role model is crucial in school at all times; in Circle Time it is essential. Personal warmth demonstrated by a good expressive vocabulary of feelings and a sensitivity to emotional needs is highly desirable. Is the teacher comfortable dealing with emotional issues? Is she a good listener? Modelling is a powerful learning tool. When children see the teacher behaving in the ways focused on in the group, they are much more inclined to understand and try new skills.

Teachers always need the ability to express themselves in a simple organised manner; never more so than in Circle Time. Lectures are avoided. The golden rule is short and concise verbal input, with active participation by everyone. This input will be most effective when it is seen by the children as a guide, not a judge, pointing out options without labelling them right or wrong, good or bad. Good teachers lead without coercion, without taking the credit, without being possessive, and in a nourishing manner.

Perhaps the most important of all is the ability to connect with the child in one's adult self. Roald Dahl had the gift of experiencing life through the eyes and ears of a child and for that he will be remembered by many.

Circle Time's success comes from establishing excellent relationships between teacher and children. Those who imagine it has to have a "mummsy", "lovey-dovey", "goody-goody" approach are quite mistaken. Here are some opinions from teachers who conduct Circle Times:

"I think the majority of teachers believe that being positive, honest and fair with children is fundamental to good classroom practice. Circle Time and the special day procedure give teachers a vehicle, a means to carry out those beliefs in a structured and controlled way."

"It has increased my awareness of what matters to children and how they see things."

"It makes them feel important. I discovered all sorts of things about them."

For you to do

1. Sit on the floor and ask a colleague to stand, look down at you and talk about something in a very detached way, asking for no questions or comments and making no real contact. Keep looking up!
2. Ask your colleague to sit on the floor with you, make good eye contact, telling you the same as above, but asking for your questions and comments and making you as involved as possible.
3. Watch your feelings and discuss the difference.

A summary of a discussion on behaviour by a class of 10/11 year old children

We talked about how we think other people see certain things that we do. Some things were seen as weak, and some were seen as strong. (G stands for Good, B stands for Bad. Some things were seen as both Good and Bad.)

Strong		Weak	
Swearing	B	Moaning	B
Fighting in different ways	B	Getting cross	B
Telling	G/B	Hit and run	B
Walking away	G	Telling	G/B
Ignoring	G	Running away	B
Threatening	B	Chickening out	B
Calling names	B	Threatening	B
Crying	G/B	Calling names	B
Sticking together	G	Crying	G/B
Forgiving	G	Giving up	B
		Revenge	B

Here are the strong and good things we can aim at:

1. Walk away from trouble.
2. It's right to tell, sometimes.
3. Ignore provocation.
4. Stick together with your friends in good and bad times.
5. Forgive someone who's done something wrong to you.
6. It's good to cry sometimes.

Here are the weak and bad things we can try and miss:

moaning,   getting cross,   hitting and running,
telling tales,   running away,   chickening out of things,
threatening people,   calling names,   giving up,
taking revenge against someone.

The whole school approach

The circle is the shape of harmony.
Twylah Nitsch, an elder of the Soneca tribe of North American Indians

What makes some schools more effective than others? There is no one formula for the creation of a successful school. Each one has its own unique character. In each case however, the overall ethos, regardless of size, building, catchment area etc., does have one thing in common - the nourishment of the self-esteem of its members.

Just as people see different things in a painting, a book or a film, so teachers when discussing Circle Times in the staffroom or in workshops see different aspects of them which they consider of value. However, whatever their age or experience, from student teachers to colleagues of long-standing, they all agree that Circle Times really do promote self-esteem in the community. Circle Times do affect what happens in all the other exchanges which take place in the school day and hopefully their message does not conflict with all the other practices that go on in the institution. It pays dividends to examine all the nooks and crannies of the organisation to root out any practices which lessen self-esteem. How are the children told to enter the building, for example, or what happens at assembly or in the playground at lunch time? Research shows that it can take years of a child's life to overcome the bad effects caused by a low functioning, negative teacher. The most casual remark which is a "put down" is often remembered long after the rest of school is forgotten. Good support systems among the staff are crucial - everyone gains.

The relationships between child and child, child and adult, adult and adult are outstanding.
extract from HMI Report on a Cambridgeshire school

Some ask if Circle Time can be justified for those who already have good self-esteem. No one can ever have too much self-esteem. Self-esteem always needs maintenance and can be further developed. It can be compared to physical health. No one can have too much. When we have good health it needs to be looked after and cherished. The same is true for our self-esteem.

Many people associate self-esteem with arrogance, boasting and bragging; these qualities are a clear indication of the lack of it. In the anxiety to overcome insecurity and to prove themselves to others, these children have to make comparisons and to compete. Good self-esteem is not about feeling superior to others because you feel better than they are, or that you can do something faster or neater.

Circle Time helps every child from the most able to the least able. Children with high academic ability often feel isolated and different, and have to cope with being regarded as a freak or teacher's favourite. They often need time and patience to help them adjust socially. When Paulo Freire went to South America in 1972 to start an adult illiteracy project he got nowhere until he realised how little people valued themselves and so set up a self-esteem programme. Teachers coping with learning difficulties in children will not get the results they work so hard for until they do the same.

Children need

to feel acceptance and understanding before giving of their best
to feel secure
to ask questions
to learn how to cope with their fears
to feel good about themselves before they can learn from you.
Cumbria Guidelines on Meeting Pupil's Special Learning Needs

For you to do

♦ Remember a time when you were a child when you were happy. Who was there?
♦ What happened?
♦ What other feelings were you experiencing?
♦ Did you feel cared for and supported and have a strong sense of security?
♦ Do you want the children in school to enjoy similar feelings?
♦ Are you willing to spend time and effort finding out and putting into effect those practices which will achieve this?
♦ If so, find colleagues who want to do this too and discuss ways you can work together.

The significance of the circle: the circle as a symbol of self.
It expresses the totality of the psyche in all its aspects, including the relationship between man and the whole of nature. Whether the symbol of the circle appears in primitive sun worship or modern religion, in myths or in dreams, in the mandala drawn by Tibetan monks . . . it always points to the single most vital aspect of life . . . its ultimate wholeness.
Roundness (the mandala motif) generally symbolises a natural wholeness. The round table, incidentally, is a well-known symbol of wholeness and plays a role in mythology
King Arthur's round table.
Aniela Jaffe, Man and His Symbols, edited Carl Jung, Picador 1978

Circle Time and the National Curriculum

Lord, when thou givest to thy servants to endeavour any great matter, grant us also to know that it is not the beginning, but the continuing of the same until it is thoroughly finished, which yieldeth true glory.

Sir Francis Drake at Plymouth

I do wish to emphasise that high self-esteem not only makes children - and adults - more responsible in their behaviour and more understanding towards others, but also brings alive qualities which give dividends in all other aspects of life, not least academic learning. To have a sense of purpose and a sense of competence manifests itself in vitality, enthusiasm, persistence and comprehension. High self-esteem is associated with high productivity and aspirations for excellent standards. Low self-esteem produces the opposite effect.

This has become quickly apparent to those teachers conducting Circle Time with their class. Here are three of the comments which have been made about it:

"When I was first introduced to Circle Time about two years ago I was impressed by its almost immediate effect. One of my early observations was about how quickly the children's speech improved. One word became ten as they experimented with words and found a variety of ways in which they could be used."

"Numerous aspects of the National Curriculum can be covered by work in Circle Time. There is stress on children being able to listen to each other, voice an opinion, and sustain an argument. Circle Time is ideal for getting children into small groups to discuss issues and report back to the group as a whole. In Circle Time children can take part as speakers and listeners with increased confidence and be actively encouraged to comment constructively. Ideas and information are re-evaluated and logical argument can be practised. By giving the children something to talk about which they know, they become active participants in their own learning. They are able to see it is their thoughts and knowledge which are being valued and sought after, that they are a valuable resource."

"Circle Time is about positive communication and interaction. The majority of the work is verbal. My experience with it has led me to believe that through this linguistically interactive process children will become better learners because they develop greater confidence and ability through experience to understand the spoken word. It will also help them 'to express themselves effectively in a variety of speaking and listening activities matching style and response to audience and purpose (National Curriculum English document: Attainment Target 1; Speaking and Listening)'."

Circle Time, behaviour and collaboration

The margins for behaviour change

1.   Current limiting behaviour

2.   Circle Time activities and skills training

3.   Self-esteem and internal motivation

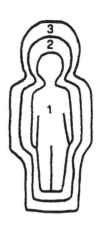

Circle Time's special strength is the effect it has on behaviour. Its value in training in human relations and interpersonal sensitivity is clear. Children learn to recognise how their emotions and actions are affected by others, and how the emotions and actions of others affect them. They begin to learn new ways of looking at things, they are prepared to experiment with new behaviours and they have the opportunity to reflect on what these new experiences mean for them. All this can happen from a very early age. It can make a major contribution to developing and sustaining a high level of self-esteem.

> *We have not yet come to grips with the social and emotional factors involved in learning and there is still a debate about how to motivate children. There is an under-researched area around collaboration; we know that you can improve performance by persuading children to co-operate, but few primary teachers are doing that.*
>
> *Professor Maurice Galton, TES, November 1991*

Circle Time provides an ideal setting where collaborative learning methods can be tried and tested. Most children would prefer to work together as a group. Working together is a privilege and it is a rare child who wants to be left out for long. However developing skills to work in a group is difficult; it does not happen by osmosis. It can be argued that learning to work together is as basic as learning to read and write and should therefore warrant the same amount of teaching time and effort.

Statements by teachers who have conducted Circle Times include:

> *"My comment is that Circle Time is a unifying influence in the class."*

> *"A later observation was about the way a collection of individuals with strong characters, not previously known for their empathy, was beginning to form into a cohesive and mutually supportive group. When this group passed on to their next teacher I wondered what would happen as their new teacher had a very different style to me. A month into the new term the teacher reported that the new class was "wonderful" and "very together" as a group."*

Circle Time is not a cloning activity; it is about empowerment. The first step towards empowerment is awareness - becoming aware of why we are like we are and why we do what we do. Completion of the statements printed below is a very valuable process and children should be encouraged to complete them often, sometimes after a particular activity, sometimes to sum up a Circle Time itself. Obviously it will depend on the age and maturity of the children but persistence of their use with even young children will soon bring rewards. The statements help them to evaluate and integrate their experiences, widening their horizons and increasing their awareness.

The list can usefully be on permanent display and the children can be reminded to use them on all sorts of occasions, especially if they keep diaries or journals.

For you to do

Keep a journal for at least a week, making daily entries recording your experiences and using these statements. At the end of the time, note any changes that have occurred in your awareness or behaviour.

I learned that I . . .

I realised that I . . .

I noticed that I . . .

I discovered that I . . .

I was surprised that I . . .

I was pleased that I . . .

I was displeased that I . . .

Circle Time and the home/school partnership

A man who has been the indisputable favourite of his mother keeps for life the feeling of a conqueror.

Sigmund Freud

Circle Time is an excellent device for drawing home/school interests together. I know of many instances where parents have noticed changes in behaviour in their children after participation in Circle Time and are naturally curious to find out what brought these about. Meetings called to explain the philosophy of Circle Time are usually well attended and received with enthusiasm. Parents quickly realise the value of giving their children a positive belief system and are usually eager for suggestions for activities which can be used at home. So, as well as promoting good relations between parents and teachers, it helps family relationships as well.

"I want to congratulate you. I thought the attendance was good and the message came across really well."

School Governor

"There are more instances of co-operation and help from parents now."

"Parents are coming in to find out what is happening in the class to make their children so keen to get there."

"Parents are asking for confirmation that the other children really did say those things about their child and are subsequently framing their Special Day Certificates."

The truest test of civilisation is not the census, nor the site of cities, nor the crops, no, but the kind of man the country turns out.

Ralph Waldo Emmerson

What the children think about Circle Time

In his school in ancient Greece, Socrates used to listen at doors. If he didn't hear laughter within five minutes he would enter the classroom to see what was wrong! Let's all use levity like yeast to lighten the necessary lessons.

Letter in TES, July 1991

It is when we are enjoying ourselves that we absorb the most. Smiles and laughter are powerful learning tools. There are always plenty of both in Circle Time, and that makes even the serious issues that are dealt with easier to handle.

It is a time which is universally popular with children. They are very perceptive about what is happening as these comments show:

"Circle Time brings us together as a class."

"I think it helps us to help, share and play with one another."

"It gives us a chance to get geared into school work."

"Circle Time is a good time because it is joyful and funny because you can say what you want and have votes."

"I think Circle Time helps us not to be shy and worried."

"It's a good way of letting the teacher know what you want and what your feelings are."

"I think Special Days are good for us because it makes us want to come to school more and enjoy what we are learning at the same time."

"Circle Time is very very very good."

Compliments and children

In School Matters, a survey of 50 London junior schools by Peter Mortimer et al, observers noted that teachers spent less than one per cent of their time giving praise. Another survey concluded that children hear about 15,000 negative statements in school per year. In a study of family life it was noted that the average child heard 16 negative statements for every positive one. Yet if children are to learn they need positive feedback 90% of the time - we all do!

I believe that the first reason for the success of the Special Day procedure is that the children know they will be appreciated and affirmed. I also believe, and there is evidence to this effect, that to help children gain high self-esteem, we need to teach them to give compliments to others. This is why the Special Day procedure is such a powerful activity, a strong daily dose of self-esteem medicine to counteract all the negative statements in the environment. I always caution teachers beginning Circle Time to expect to see change come slowly, but many notice differences in some children immediately and I'm sure it comes from taking part in this activity. It has even caused differences in parents' attitudes, as mentioned previously.

'The Special Day theme was enthusiastically received by the children and as a result they kept asking for Circle Time. The children liked what they heard about themselves especially when a child with low self-esteem realised that others liked him and were prepared to say it with the rest of the class listening.'

'A rather difficult year one child was described by the class when he was "special" as follows: 'he doesn't fight, he works hard, he helps us," ' All of which was blatantly untrue. However, for some considerable time after his special day, this is exactly how he behaved.'

'Seeing children participating in Circle Time made me realise how children can become self-confident. I would like to see Circle Time put into every junior and secondary school daily schedule. If this could be implemented it would lead the less confident children into becoming whole adults with a true belief in themselves.'

There needs to be a common self-esteem vocabulary in use throughout the school. A name for positive statements needs to be chosen which will appeal to the children's imagination. I have heard them called compliments, strokes, warm fuzzies, sparklers, builder uppers. Pick a word which appeals to the youngest and the oldest children and then make sure everyone knows what it means and that it is well used.

For you to do

1. Give a genuine, thoughtful compliment to a child who concerns you every day for two or three weeks. It doesn't matter how brief it is. Do not be put off by any initial adverse reaction.
2. Give a compliment daily to any colleague who appears to need some extra support.
3. Give compliments to all those at home, friends, shopkeepers, all you come in contact with.
4. Be aware of your feelings when you receive a compliment.

A compliment is enhanced tremendously by touch - from the gentlest touch on the arm or shoulder to the warm embrace. If words can't express it, say it with hugs.

A hug is the best gift you can give. It embraces all sizes and you can always exchange it.
Kathleen Keating, The Little Book of Hugs

Try these today!

'I'm glad you're here (in this class/in this school)'

'I like the way you . . .'

'I appreciate your help'

'That was great'

'I respect you for . . .'

'I really enjoyed doing that with you'

'That sounds a fine idea'

'I delight in your way of . . .'

'I celebrate who you are because . . .'

Stress in children

How we respond to certain events in our lives depends on our levels of self-esteem; their levels will indicate how well we feel able to deal with the problems presented to us. As adults we tend to think that we are the ones under stress but childhood brings its own pressures. Many children are under enormous amounts of stress but they seldom receive as much attention.

UNICEF commissioned reports on children in eight industrialised countries. The report on the UK was prepared by Professor Jonathan Bradshaw and the National Children's Bureau and published in 1991. Its conclusion was that during the 1980s it was children who bore the brunt of the disadvantages caused by economic difficulties. The number of children living in poverty doubled; 2.5 million children were in families with incomes at or below the supplementary income level. Many would argue however that the serious economic disadvantages a child can suffer from poverty are less important than the emotional deprivation children may experience when not brought up in a two-parent family. Today one in four children can expect to see their parents divorced - a five hundred per cent increase since 1980. Research shows clear evidence of the adverse effects of that experience.

A less obvious but major reason for stress in children derives from a feeling that they have no power in their lives, with little control over their days, always doing things according to someone else's timetable. Sometimes in an effort to satisfy the unrealistic ambitions of parents they will have a constant fear of failure, which will certainly induce stress. There are many reasons for its onset.

Stress can make us both physically and mentally ill. Warning signals in children include inability to sleep, bad dreams, listlessness, a previously sociable child becoming reclusive, or becoming aggressive in a way that is out of character. Doctors say that there is an increased incidence of high blood pressure in children under seven.

So introducing children to strategies to cope with stress helps in both the short- and long-term, dealing with immediate concerns and imparting a knowledge about how to deal with difficulties later in life. Relaxation and visualisation is only part of the solution, however. A great deal can be done to reduce stress by allowing children to talk and Circle Time is the obvious forum, a safe, non-judgmental environment.

Where children are anxious or distressed they need to believe that they attend a 'listening school' and that the 'personal voice' of individual children is valued and respected. For this to happen (from infants to top juniors and beyond) discussion needs to occupy a regular place in the school timetable. Contexts for speaking and listening need to be established within every classroom.

BBC Education, Teaching Today

Circle Times will lessen the need for one to one exchanges with troubled children but there will always be some children who require this attention.

Exercises which may be used within any Circle Time to promote a sense of well-being are described on pages 109 - 113. Use the exercises often. Their value should not be judged by doing them only once. The more frequently they are done the more the children become accustomed to them and benefit from them. Physical fitness demands regular attention to exercise and diet. Mental well-being and a sense of self-esteem also justifies time and effort.

There is much of value in doing visualisations with children. Apart from the sense of calmness which is achieved they lead to increased self-confidence and self-acceptance. As well as doing them in Circle Times, a good time to use them can be before creative writing and art lessons, or with an appropriate script where work is to be done in assessment conditions. Visualisations are also vastly superior to giving grim negative 'lectures' about poor behaviour when the aim is to change attitudes and encourage a positive approach.

A Sense of Magic

Child:	*Can I have a pencil?*
Teacher:	*Is there something else you need to say?*
Child:	Pause . . .
Teacher:	*Now what is the magic word you say when you want something?*
Child:	(with enthusiasm) *Abracadabra!*

Children love magic and mystery so it was with a sense of excited anticipation that the children entered their classroom on Monday morning. On the previous Friday afternoon each child had written their name on a small piece of paper, pushed the piece of paper into their own balloon and blown it up. The balloons were then suspended in a cluster from the ceiling.

I sat on the floor, shoes off, in a space that had been cleared of desks. As the children came in, I greeted each one by name and gestured to them to join me. Soon a circle was formed. I invited all the children to look round it, catch the eye of anyone they had not yet seen and to give that person a friendly wave or smile.

There was then a hush. What next? "What about making some noise?" My invitation was readily accepted. "Well then this is what we do." We stood, bent our knees and touched the floor with only the ends of our toes and the tips of our fingers. As we slowly unravelled and straightened up, our hum got louder and louder and when we were at full-stretch we jumped as high as we could and yelled as loudly as possible. We did this three times, making more noise each time - "So that the whole school can hear us!"

We sat down. We looked at each other. There was a comfortable feeling in the room. Circle Time had begun.

> *While parents possess the original key to their children's experiences, the spare key is held by the teachers.*
>
> *Haim Ginott: Teacher and Child*

Children need to feel secure, know that they are appreciated as individuals, and have a real sense of belonging to a group: these are the first three basic requirements for building self-esteem, and I was determined that school should provide them. Too many children walk into school each day with a less-than-acceptable level of self-esteem as is evident from their attitudes, behaviours and preoccupations. I decided that there was to be something in this session for everyone; the whole class would be together without interruptions, and it would start every school day.

The Ingredients
There is a basic list of ingredients which build up the elements of self-esteem, but the recipe can be changed daily as long as the whole diet is dealt with over a period. Circle Time is never dull. There are many varied and interesting activities, and children will soon become involved in what is done each day. The choice is wide.

The ingredients include:

- 'Special Day' procedure
- rounds
- discussions and listening experiences
- games and energisers
- role-play, movement and dance
- drawing, painting, art and craft
- touch-and-trust experiences
- relaxation and meditation techniques
- guided imagery and visualisation work
- journals, observation books, success diaries.

The elements of self-esteem are best tackled sequentially:

- a sense of security
- a sense of identity
- a sense of belonging
- a sense of purpose
- a sense of competence.

It is vital that a sense of security be firmly established at the beginning.

When the routines are established and the theory understood, teachers can diagnose elements that are lacking in individual children, and strategies can be devised and built into Circle Time which will help particular pupils.

All the ingredients (except the Special Day procedure) can be blended in any number of ways to promote the five elements listed above. These elements can be dealt with in a series of Circle Time sessions:

getting started...	building a supportive environment
self-identity...	recognising that each child is unique and has a special contribution to make to life
relating...	examining the value of friendship and co-operation
feelings...	becoming aware of feelings, and understanding them, and learning how to handle them
stress...	dealing with worry, anxiety, pressure
conflict...	the resolution of problems into win-win situations
goal-setting...	the promotion of self-correction and self-direction.

The Special Day

This is a wonderful way to help a child gain a sense of security, identity and belonging: I have not met, or heard of, a child refuse the opportunity to have a Special Day. Children all look forward to them immensely and seem to remember them vividly. I overheard two eight-year-old boys sitting in the circle when one had just discovered it was his turn on that day: "It's Wednesday today and it was a Wednesday last time."; "Mine was on a Friday.".
I have never known a child to complain about having to wait for a turn, or that the turn was over. All children know they will get a turn, although they have the excitement of not knowing when, and once it is over they know that their turn will come again. There are enough days in a term for each child in an average-size class to have two Special Days per term, six per year. It is like having six really good birthdays every year!

If we can help children to think positively about themselves, and to learn how they can take charge of their own lives, they will come to realise they can have a Special Day every day. If we can help pupils to understand their own uniqueness:

♦ What have a snowflake and a fingerprint in common?
♦ Every one is unique.
♦ What else is unique and special?
♦ Every child; each one of us.

Procedure

The group should be sitting in a circle and a child randomly selected. One method is to give out balloons the day before Circle Time begins, one to each child. Before they are blown up and suspended from the ceiling, the child writes his name on a small piece of paper and drops it inside. The following day when everyone is ready, the pin is flourished, the balloon is popped and out drops the name of the child to have a Special Day.

When the balloons are finished the children can choose their own means of selection. Advent-type calendars, with names behind the windows, are popular, so are panels of faces with names under the tongues. Names pushed into straws can be used, as can examples of children's writing put into unmarked envelopes which are pinned to the wall. A longer way is for children to draw a self-portrait on one side of paper, and riddles about themselves on the other. One can be selected daily, the portrait shown and the riddles read out while the group guesses who it is. The selection is usually made by the child who had the Special Day on the previous day.

The child for today (the Special Day child) is invited into the centre of the circle and presented with a badge or token of some kind on behalf of the group. These badges can be home-made or there are some appropriate commercial ones. Some children prefer to make their own. Children like wearing them. Suggested words for badges: "Today is special!" and "I am great!"

Name posters are one way of recording the Special Day comments; they look attractive displayed round the room.

Jumps high
Always helpful
My friend
Easy to be with
Skilled at soccer

Able to work well
Never loses her temper
Nice to go home with
Eager to help me

Keeps friends
Empathic
Likeable
Looks after her pets
You trust her

Either now or later, get the group to give the child a standing ovation - 30 seconds of clapping, cheering and whistles, offered with energy and enthusiasm! How many of us have this experience even once in a lifetime, and yet we all deserve it!

The Special Day child then sits in the middle of the circle and receives the positive comments of the others in the group. These remarks and comments should be prefaced with "I think ... " or "I believe..." etc., which stops the hearing child denying them at either a conscious or subconscious level. A great sense of belonging is given, and the Special Day child feels much appreciated, for example, "He said he liked my smile", "She said I was a nice person to be with".

Until the class gets used to the idea it can be wise to invite the Special Day child to wait outside the door while a rehearsal takes place This gives the adult a chance to hear the remarks beforehand and to prompt when necessary. It's the only time I know when children are gladly sent to stand outside the door! Comments should be recorded and presented for the child to keep (see page 11). Many of these may come to occupy a proud place in the bedroom at home. It is important because most of us have difficulty letting in the good things said about us.

The Special Day child should then be invited to disclose something about themselves, for example, something he likes doing, making, collecting, reading, watching or eating. This will give a further feeling of affiliation to the group. Even though it is difficult for most, the child should also be encouraged to disclose something he has done or made of which he is pleased and proud: it is not bragging or boasting, it is not making comparisons with others; it does enhance self-esteem. Another approach is to have a list of qualities on display, for example, "punctual", "quick-thinking", "persevering", and ask the children to tell the Special Day child which of those qualities apply to that child. The list acts as a reminder of some words to use. It can be added to all the time.

At this point a Circle Time round and/or a short discussion take place.

A Circle Time round begins with a sentence stem like: "The first thought I had when I knew it was going to be my Special Day was . . . ".

Circle Time discussion sessions are the times when children share with each other their thoughts, feelings, aspirations etc.

As part of the session a discussion could take place, involving as many group members as possible, which considers possible new ways that the Special Day child may like to behave this day. A risk, taken with wisdom and skill, is a sure-fire way to enhance self-esteem. This Special Day routine, with its provision of an aware, caring environment, can be just what a child with a long record of failure and frustration needs, to make a new beginning. An introverted child could be encouraged to be more assertive knowing that the group is aware of his efforts and will be supportive. If a child can try out a new way of behaviour and break an old pattern which is holding back his true potential, this can lead to a realisation of being in control of his life.

All children love to claim the privileges which are available on Special Days. Sitting in a specifi-cally arranged row of chairs (remember there is one child from each class) at assembly is something they invariably enjoy. They can ask to use the limited play equipment (which does away with the need to decide who can use it) and can choose a game to be played, either at Circle Time or later in the day. They can ask for a cup of tea or coffee from the staffroom at break. Their favourite lesson can be included in the day's timetable. No reasonable request will be refused. Some children offer to be friendly or help children they do not normally associate with. It encourages initiative and gives confidence to ask for what is wanted.

The Special Day child can request a "clap please". This can be said in class at any reasonable time during the day, and a quick round of applause will follow. I have never known it to be abused, and it certainly brings lots of smiles.

Special Days are good for adults too. They can be carried out in the classroom (you will find that children will want to arrange them as a surprise and will rig the selection procedure to achieve it) and in the staffroom. It's a really good experience when staff can say how much they appreciate each other. The privileges that can be claimed carry endless possibilities!

> *People who feel good about themselves produce good results.*
> **S Johnson and K Blanchard: The One Minute Manager**

For you to do
Take time to do this validation exercise with a colleague. (How difficult it is, people say, but how worthwhile, they add.)

> Partner A has three minutes to talk about all the things which make her a good teacher, and what she is good at doing in school. If she dries up, her partner will say each time "Tell me more, please", and at full time, for at least one minute, will give A a verbal pat on the back, e.g. "It sounds to me as if you really do . . . well, and that you get a lot of satisfaction from it," etc. - B generally shows appreciation for A.
>
> B then takes a turn.
>
> At the end, if you feel like it, give each other a hug.

Special Day

For

Today is

The reasons people like me are:

Rounds

A round is an excellent way of starting Circle Time. It is a highly visible way of bringing the children together at the beginning of the day, acknowledging each one's membership of the group and reminding them of the value of their relationship to others.

When a group is new it is often useful to begin with a round which includes each person's name, for example, "My name is . . . and today I . . ."; this is a good way of making a new member feel welcome, and visitors can be included easily into the group.

Sentence stems which are left open for each child to complete, are a very powerful tool for helping the teachers to appreciate children's needs. Many statements that are made will lead to a better understanding of the child.

It is better not to question or comment on statements during the round. If need be, issues can be dealt with at the end, or left for future class or small group discussions, or be discussed with the child privately.

The facilitator should always start. A sentence stem could be, "Today I intend to be friendly by . . ." . . pause . . now complete the stem, " . . . giving everyone I meet a smile". Then repeat the stem, look at the child on the left or right, and they continue the round. Some children will say "Pass" mainly because they need more time to think. They can be returned to at the end. Others need gentle encouragement. The number of passes diminishes as the group is established. Children that feel safe love this opportunity to speak to the class and it is usually high-quality listening time.

For you to do

Write the endings to these statements with the first thought that comes to mind. Read them back slowly or discuss them with a trusted colleague. Did you discover anything?

> I'm happiest when . . .
> I feel saddest when . . .
> I feel most important when . . .
> I get angry when . . .
> A thought I keep having is . . .
> My friends are . . .
> I don't like people who . . .
> When someone tells me they like me I . . .
> I appreciate . . .
> I pretend to be . . . when really I'm . . .
> Something I do well is . . .
> Something I'm getting better at is . . .
> I have difficulty in dealing with . . .
> I can help other people to . . .
> Strong independent people . . .

Some rounds

Rounds can often be used as an introduction or linked to the other activities that will take place in the Circle Time, for example, a sentence stem about animals can lead on to interesting movement and body work, a stem about what I'd like to be can spark lively discussions on ambitions, careers, and the family system:

> When I woke this morning my first thought was . . .
> As I walked to school today I was thinking of . . .
> When someone says something nice/nasty to me I feel . . .
> My favourite place at home is . . .
> My favourite place to play is . . .
> I feel really good/bad when . . .
> If I were a giant I would . . .
> If I were an animal/fruit/toy I would be a . . .
> If I could do anything I wanted I would . . .
> I hope that . . .
> I like it /don't like it when . . .
> I like/don't like people who . . .
> If I could only have one thing (as much as I wanted) to eat/drink for the
>   rest of the week I would choose . . .
> Today I hope I shall be able to . . .
> Today I would like to help a person/people to . . .
> Today I would like someone to help me to . . .
> I was very happy/sad/angry/scared when once . . .
> I shall always remember the first time I . . .
> If I could be invisible I would . . .
> I would like the magic ring that . . .
> School would be better if . . .
> One of the best things about me is . . .
> I like going to . . .
> If I were the/a teacher I would . . .
> I laugh when . . .

The last sentence stem can lead on to a laughing competition - who has the most contagious laugh? Making space for sharing jokes is popular. Apart from the need to share fun and humour, the ability to tell a story properly in order to get an appropriate reaction is a skill that needs practising.

For you to do
   ◆ Ask yourself how you feel when you smile?
   ◆ Does it make any difference to the way you do your work?

Discussions

Circle Time is an excellent forum for discussion. Discussions can benefit children in many ways. For example, children often have the mistaken belief that they alone experience the stresses of abuse, domestic violence, divorce, sibling rivalry, fear of failure, teasing, bullying, thinking themselves unattractive and so on. Discovering that they share the same longings, difficulties, conflicts and doubts enhances their self-esteem. Children will learn how to share and be comfortable with their feelings and this, in turn, may enable them to resist the increasing problems of depression, drugs and alcohol.

Discussions are most successful in small groups, later the class group is used for feedback and summing up. The way the small groups are formed is important. For forming groups most of the time, random groupings, rather than friendships should be used. This can be done in many ways, for example, by asking the children to find others born in the same month, or who have the same initials or who are wearing different/the same colours. Three is the best psychological number for a group of this nature - a triad. Sometimes it is more appropriate to bring two triads together for feedback rather than immediately reforming the big group. The use of these triads can be extended to activities other than those done in Circle Time, known as the Buddy System, it is a very powerful dynamic for encouraging a flourishing class atmosphere.

Circle Time is a good place for developing listening skills. Such skills are valuable in all relationships and, by and large, children do not get enough positive attention. Circle Time is a good opportunity for the shy and more isolated child to express himself, and be heard. Children can be told about the Melanesians who used a conch shell; the one who held it spoke while everyone else listened. A beanbag makes a useful substitute, or something brought specially from home.

Brainstorming

Brainstorming is a valuable method to introduce to the class or group. A brainstorming session aims to generate ideas from a main theme and no matter how far-fetched, or trivial, the ideas, the session will undoubtedly generate a lot of energy and good-natured argument.

For you to do

1. Think of a time when you felt that someone wasn't listening to you. What did the other person do or say?
2. Think of a time when you felt that someone was listening to you. What did the other person do or say?
3. What conditions do you need in order to be able to listen?
4. What do you say, do or feel when you need to get the agreement of someone on an issue important to you?
5. Discuss in a triad!

Discussion during Circle Time allows children to discover mutual likes and dislikes in sport, hobbies, music and the arts. Fighting, teasing, racial and gender incidents all get a good airing, and things said in Circle Time discussions can go a long way towards reducing the conflict and unpleasant behaviour found in most schools.

For example, here is a list made by a class of nine to eleven-year-olds after a discussion which arose spontaneously from a remark made by one of the children:

Acceptable and non-acceptable punishments received at home

Non-acceptable

Slapped around face and head
Beaten with the dog's stick
Mouthful of cod liver oil to swallow
Mouthful of washing-up liquid (not to swallow)
Mouthful of washing-up liquid (forced to swallow)
Wash out mouth with soap
Locked in room with no food or drink.

Acceptable

Slapped anywhere but face or head
Locked in room between meals
No television
No computer
Not allowed to play
No puddings
No sweets
No pocket money
Ignored.

School and classroom organisation make good topics for debate. Where children are involved in making rules and setting standards they are more likely to follow them. Every opportunity should be taken in schools to empower children to take responsibility for themselves.

It should be understood that the rules must be based on truth, trust, responsibility, active listening and no put-downs. For those who find it difficult to keep set rules and standards, there are many strategies available which will not diminish self-esteem and yet have the desired result. Sanctions should always be appropriate to the offence and be dealt with privately.

Rules negotiated by a group of eleven-year-olds

1. Listen to what other people say.
2. Don't be nasty to each other.
3. No talking when someone else is talking.
4. Be kind to each other and give support.
5. If all you can say is something unpleasant, don't say anything.
6. If people don't want to say anything they don't have to.
7. Don't laugh at what other people say.
8. Think before you ask a question.

Curriculum Guidance 5 Health Education, National Curriculum Council 1990

A Sense of Security

Only a child who feels safe dares to grow forward healthily. His safety needs must be gratified.
Abraham Maslow: Towards a Psychology of Being

A child with a good sense of security:

- feels safe enough to take limited risks and explore new ideas and places
- has a secure, strong relationship with a significant other
- is at ease and is comfortable with others
- is calm and centred
- can cope with change.

A child with a poor sense of security:

- is unhappy with new experiences and situations
- is withdrawn and has little contact with people
- is looking for someone to trust and depend on
- is often fearful and worried and shows this by tics (spasmodic twitching) and habits like biting nails, thumb-sucking and pulling at hair
- is seeking to establish safety by having clear limits and boundaries.

For you to do

Listen to children talking and see if you can identify those with, and those without, a sense of security, for example, "I like school; the teachers are very kind and helpful", "I don't understand what I'm supposed to do". Compare the successes in schoolwork of these different children, watch how often they take risks. Observe their relationships with others.

A Sense of identity

When a man no longer confuses himself with the definition that others have given him, he is at once universal and unique.

Alan Watts: Psychotherapy East and West

A child who has a good sense of identity:
- knows that others think he is special
- is imaginative, creative and able to express himself
- speaks positively about himself and others
- has a keen awareness of his own capabilities, attitudes and physical characteristics
- understands his feelings and how to deal with them.

A child with a poor sense of identity:
- speaks negatively about himself and others
- is rarely imaginative or creative and finds communication difficult
- conforms to other's ideas and opinions and is dependent on adults
- may seek attention by misbehaving and will be undaunted by reprimands
- will be seeking to prove uniqueness, however negative.

For you to do
Listen to children talking and see if you can identify those with, and those without, a sense of identity, for example, "I've brought my collection of stamps to show you", "I can't think of anything I like".

A Sense of Belonging

To identify with and feel with another is marvellous . . . those closely shared feelings are a special part of the bond between people.

Judith Brown: I only want what's best for you

A child who has a good sense of belonging:

♦ enjoys friendship, co-operates well
♦ communicates well and is comfortable with others
♦ knows that his opinions are listened to, and that he is wanted and liked
♦ is empathic, compassionate and sensitive.

A child with a poor sense of belonging:

♦ is uncomfortable with others and will either withdraw and become a "loner" or will always demand attention
♦ communicates badly, either with reluctance or at inappropriate times
♦ relies on shyness or boasting to gain approval
♦ feels undervalued so will reject others and be insensitive to their needs
♦ is struggling, either through aggression or separation, to be appreciated and respected by others.

For you to do

Listen to children talking and see if you can identify those with, and those without, a sense of belonging, for example, "You can borrow my felt tips", "There's never anyone to play with."

A sense of purpose

The nice thing about mistakes is that they don't have to be permanent.
Spencer Tracy, in the film about Thomas Alvar Edison. Edison made 9000 attempts before
he succeeded in making a light bulb work .

A child who has a good sense of purpose:
- Is self motivated and will set goals for herself
- Will try new ventures with enthusiasm
- Has the determination to persevere and to succeed
- Will ask for help and advice when appropriate
- Accepts encouragement comfortably.

A child with a poor sense of purpose:
- Will not risk the effort and possible failure sets impossible targets and unrealistic goals
- Gives up quickly
- Shows little initiative
- Needs to be persuaded, cajoled, coerced.

For you to do
Listen to children talking and see if you can identify those with, and those without a sense of purpose, for example, 'I'm improving with practice.' 'Will you help me to get the equipment I need to do this?' 'I don't want to do this.' 'Do I have to?,"

A sense of competence

The only way to succeed in life is to take off more than you can chew and then arrange with the mind to do it well.

Kenny Everett on TELEVISION AM, November 1991

A child who has a good sense of competence:

- is able to make choices and take decisions
- will give support to others and is willing to share
- takes responsibility for her own actions
- can cope with setbacks and learn from them
- is able to acknowledge the strengths and accomplishments of herself and others.

A child with a poor sense of competence:

- needs constant external reward and has a helpless attitude
- is a poor loser and will blame others
- avoids responsibility and is reluctant to try new ventures
- is likely to be critical of any achievements of herself and others.

For you to do:

Listen to children talking and see if you can identify those with and those without a sense of competence: for example 'I'm really proud of this model I've made, I can see where I went wrong and shall not repeat it.' 'Why are things so hard?' '1 didn't do it.'

How to use this Resource

It is suggested that you use the five sections in the order presented. Children need to feel secure before they can move on to other competencies. Experienced users will, as they become familiar with the resource, modify the activities to suit the needs and development of the young people.

There are five major sections of activities
1. Security
2. Identity
3. Belonging
4. Purpose
5. Competency.

There is a sixth section
6. Well-being
which can be used at any time during the programme. They are planned to alleviate stress and encourage a sense of well-being.

Each section has a number of separate Circle Time sessions.

Key to icons

The icons below help to identify each activity with its source section.

 Choosing the Special Day child

Round - a good way to start Circle Time

 Discussion in the Circle

Game - raises energy/fun level

 Activity - a bit like a game

Group yell - a real energiser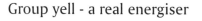

 Time to make physical contact

Plan the day - sum up

Circle Time to promote a sense of security

Circle Time to promote a sense of security 1

Opening Round

"Good morning, everyone.
A special person in my life is . . . ."
or
"Someone I really like to be with . . . ."
(The completion can be either a name or a relationship.)

Selection of child

Hello name game

Use a cushion or beanbag to throw across the circle to someone, as you do so say the person's name preceded by a greeting, like, "Hi", "Hello", "Good morning". Encourage the children to think of their own greetings. These are simple but positive statements, and there should be good eye contact. Some children have nicknames which they like and are known only to a few friends. They can be invited to share these with the group.

Be sure that everyone is included. Tell the children that if there is someone whose name they do not know, to ask for it, and then throw the cushion to that person.

Sitting is the most suitable position for most Circle Time activities, however, this game is done most effectively standing. One version, which has the merit of speed, is to sit down when you've thrown the cushion. It can then be played against the clock, but the cushion has to be thrown across the circle and not passed to a neighbour.

Introduce the discussion by asking the whole group the following question: "If you are meeting someone for the first time what do you think you should get to know about them?" Then prompt them, if necessary, with some of the following questions: "What do teachers want to know about you when you start school? If you have ever moved into a new house, how do you get to know your neighbours? What is the first thing you say to them? If a new child comes into the class what do you think you would know about them by the end of the first day? By the end of the term? What would you like them to know about you? Meeting a new person can be a real adventure. You may be talking to someone who is going to become your best friend for the rest of you life!"

Choosing a partner

"Look around the circle and decide on a few people who you do not know very well. Perhaps the ones who you don't know if they have a pet or not, or what they like to do on Saturdays. Get up and go and ask one of them to be your partner. Find a space where you can sit next to each other, but as far away from everyone else as possible."

or

"I would like you to get up and see if you can find one of the people in the group who lives the furthest away from you. Ask that person to be your partner and then find a space where you can sit next to each other, but as far away from everyone else as possible."

or

"I would like you to get up and find a partner who you have not spoken to since yesterday. With your partner find a space . . ."

Distribute interview sheets (page 49) and pencils.

"Decide which of you will be A and which B. Hands up A. Hands up B. A will be the interviewer first and will ask B the questions on the sheet. Either write the answers down or remember in your head, whichever is easier. You don't have to ask the questions in that order (if there are any children with reading difficulties, this is the time to read them aloud), and you can ask other questions if you wish. Bs do not have to answer any questions they don't wish to. Is that clear? Any questions?

"I am going to give you a few minutes (your decisions will depend on maturity of children) then I shall ask if you have had enough time.

"In a little while it will be time to change over and for B to be the interviewer. When we have all finished I shall ask you to introduce your partner to the group."

It is important not to rush this activity. Be ready to encourage some of the children. The slow starters often become the most involved.

When the interviewing has finished, the partners can introduce each other to the group. This activity can also be done in triads, two children sharing the questioning of the third. This method takes the pressure off reporting back to the group. This is a time-consuming activity, but very worthwhile, especially at the beginning of a school year or the formation of a new group.

At the end tell them that you have planned an activity on which they can work together that day so that they can get to know even more about each other.

 All hold hands and do a lighthouse. Remind children that the light from a lighthouse shines in order to help people. It shines in a friendly way helping everyone that is near it. Ask everyone to look around the circle, make eye contact with some, and smile. This should be a quick activity and done silently. It stops when the hands are parted, which the teacher initiates.

At the end of each Circle Time (if it's done at the beginning of the day) before anyone gets up, take the opportunity to announce what the plan for the rest of the day will be, to involve the children in the organisation, to remind them of equipment needed and where to find it, to tell them where they need to be at particular times, for example, appointments for doctors or swimming lessons. Point out the rules which have been jointly agreed and are displayed so that everyone can have a happy and productive day. Do the children have any questions or comments?

For you to do

Recall the assumptions you made when you saw some people for the first time. Think of people you like and know well. Remember the circumstances of your first meeting with them. Who spoke first? What was said?

Ask Your Partner:-

What is your full name?

Do you have a nickname?

What do you like to be called?

How old are you?

When is your birthday?

Who do you live with?

What are their names?

If you have brothers and sisters how old are they?

Where do you live?

How long have you lived there?

How do you get to school - walking, bicycle, bus, car?

What are your interests outside school?

Do you belong to any clubs, teams?

What games do you like?

What are your favourite television programmes?

Do you read any comics; if so which ones?

Do you borrow books from the local library?

Do you have pocket money; if so how much?

Do you have to do anything for your pocket money?

Did you go away on holiday this year?

If you could go anywhere in the world you wanted to next year, where would you go?
    Who would you go with?

If you could be any age, what age would you like to be?

Do you wish you had a larger family or a smaller family, or is your family just the right
    size?

Do you ever get teased? Do you ever tease others?

Will you smoke when you grow up? Why?

If there is one thing you could change, what would it be?

Who is the best teacher you have ever had? Why?

Do you enjoy being at school? Is there anything you would like to change about school?

Is there one thing which you would like to learn how to do better?

There will be lots of other questions you can think of. Remember, they should only be
    ones which you wouldn't mind someone asking you.

The person being asked the questions can always say "Pass" if he or she wants to.

Circle Time to promote a sense of security 2

Opening Round

"I think the most important rule that we have in school is . . . ."

Selection of child

A child goes outside the room and returns to guess who changed places in the interim. Lots of variations can make it easier or harder and therefore a safe risk for some and a bigger challenge for others.

Generate the discussion by using the following ideas as prompts. "What are rules, and why do we have them? Imagine a school with no rules. What would be the advantages and disadvantages? Do all schools have the same rules? Has anyone experience of another school?"

"Rules are best made by the people to whom they will apply. Are the laws in China or Japan the same as in this country? Can you imagine the government in those countries telling us about traffic laws?" Ask for examples.

"So what are our school rules?" The teacher or a volunteer writes them on a list as they are offered and adds any not mentioned.

"School rules apply to everyone in this school, but we as a group need our own rules. We call them ground rules or basic rules and they must apply to everyone. By respecting the ground rules we have set ourselves we can feel safe and secure within our group.

"Everyone of us is unique, as we know. I know what rules I would like, but they might not be the ones you want, so let's find out what each other's rules would be.

"I want you to work with two other people and make a list of the rules you would like. After a little while we'll come back together and make a combined list."

A free choice of partners is recommended for this activity.

At the end, receive all suggestions for rules without comment. Invite children to discuss them. Remind them of the advantages of having few rules. Can they recommend any rules that could be pruned from the list?

Finally, ask if all the rules on the list can be agreed unanimously. Remind them of the English system of majority votes and the ways we make laws. Ask that everyone accepts the final list, a show of hands or similar gesture is helpful, and then say that these ground rules operate from this time on. For example, Circle Time rules:

1.   Only one person at a time.
2.   Don't spoil anyone's fun.
3.   Have fun yourself!

All hold hands and do a lighthouse. Remind children that the light from a lighthouse shines in order to help people. It shines in a friendly way helping everyone that is near it. Ask everyone to look around the circle, make eye contact with some, and smile. This should be a quick activity and done silently. Announce that everyone within range of the light knows the Circle Time rules just agreed upon.

At the end of each Circle Time (if it's done at the beginning of the day) before anyone gets up, take the opportunity to announce what the plan for the rest of the day will be, to involve the children in the organisation, to remind them of equipment needed and where to find it, to tell them where they need to be at particular times, for example, appointments for doctors or swimming lessons. Point out the rules which have been jointly agreed and are on display so that everyone can have a happy and productive day. Do the children have any questions now? Any comments?

Circle Time to promote a sense of security 3

Opening Round

"My name is . . . and today I wish . . . ."

Selection of child

Who is this?

A child volunteers to sit in front of another in the circle but not before the latter has shut his eyes. He keeps them closed, stretches his arms out and uses his hands to feel the head and features of the other, trying to guess who it is.

Make sure everyone gets a turn, but not necessarily on the same day. (Can be done two or three couples at a time.)

"Today I'm going to give each of you a piece of paper and I would like you to go and sit where you can write on it without being overlooked."

The group disperses and a piece of paper is distributed to each child.

"This game is called secrets. I would like you to think of a secret which you are willing to share with this group. You write it on this paper, but you do not put your name on it. What sort of secrets should you write? You can say things like what you really hate, or what you like very much, or what you are afraid of. People have all kinds of secrets. I will give you a minute to think. When you have written your secrets we jumble all the paper up in this box. Sitting in a circle I shall take out one at a time and read it to the group. Even if I recognise the writing I shall never reveal the author's name. What we do then is to guess who wrote it. It will remain up to you to decide if you tell us it is your secret; I hope you will feel able to."

In this activity it is important for teachers to participate. Disclosing an anxiety will certainly help children to share their own. The secrets are read out and shared. At the end pose the question: "How did you feel sharing your secret with us?" Give some time for discussion.

All hold hands and do a lighthouse. Remind children that the light from a lighthouse shines in order to help people. It shines in a friendly way helping everyone that is near it. Ask everyone to look around the circle, make eye contact with some, and smile. This should be a quick activity and done silently. It stops when the hands are parted, which the teacher initiates.

At the end of each Circle Time (if it's done at the beginning of the day) before anyone gets up, take the opportunity to announce what the plan for the rest of the day will be, to involve the children in the organisation, to remind them of equipment needed and where to find it, to tell them where they need to be at particular times, for example, appointments for doctors or swimming lessons. Point out the rules which have been jointly agreed and are on display so that everyone can have a happy and productive day. Do the children have any questions now? Any comments?

Circle Time to promote a sense of security 4

Opening Round

"Good morning everyone. If I were the king/queen/prime minister I would . . . ."

Selection of child

Name game

The child on the left begins by saying his name, for example "My name is John". The child on his left then says "Your name is John, I am Kate". The next one says "You are John, you are Kate and I am Sarah", and so on.

It's absolutely acceptable if someone cannot remember and has to ask to be reminded of someone's name - except for you! Your turn is last of course, and you can make a big fuss of each child as you say their name - you could get up and shake each one by the hand, or pretend to get mixed up, or prefix each name with "the great" etc. This is a good opportunity to say that you appreciate them all.

Produce a ball of string or wool. Hold the end and make a personal disclosure of some kind, for example "The name of the book I am reading at the moment is . . .", or "I am looking forward to doing . . . with . . .", then pass the ball to someone else who does the same, and so on, creating a web around the circle.

As the ball is rewound children can be asked if they can remember who said what.

All hold hands and do a lighthouse. Remind children that the light from a lighthouse shines in order to help people. It shines in a friendly way helping everyone that is near it. Ask everyone to look around the circle, make eye contact with some, and smile. This should be a quick activity and done silently. It stops when the hands are parted, which the teacher initiates.

At the end of each Circle Time (if it's done at the beginning of the day) before anyone gets up, take the opportunity to announce what the plan for the rest of the day will be, to involve the children in the organisation, to remind them of equipment needed and where to find it, to tell them where they need to be at particular times, for example, appointments for doctors or swimming lessons. Point out the rules which have been jointly agreed and are on display so that everyone can have a happy and productive day. Do the children have any questions now? Any comments?

Circle Time to promote a sense of identity

Circle Time to promote a sense of identity 1

A Sense of Magic.

Children love magic and mystery so it was with a sense of excited anticipation that the children entered their classroom on Monday morning. On the previous Friday afternoon each child had written their name on a small piece of paper, pushed the piece of paper into their own balloon and blown it up. The balloons were then suspended in a cluster from the ceiling.

I sat on the floor, shoes off, in a space that had been cleared of desks. As the children came in, I greeted each one by name and gestured to them to join me. Soon a circle was formed. I invited all the children to look round it, catch the eye of anyone they had not yet seen and to give that person a friendly wave or smile.

There was then a hush. What next? "What about making some noise?" My invitation was readily accepted. "Well then this is what we do." We stood, bent our knees and touched the floor with only the ends of our toes and the tips of our fingers. As we slowly unravelled and straightened up, our hum got louder and louder and when we were at full-stretch we jumped as high as we could and yelled as loudly as possible. We did this three times, making more noise each time - "So that the whole school can hear us!"

We sat down. We looked at each other. There was a comfortable feeling in the room. Circle Time had begun.

A round
"One of the best things that has ever happened to me is when . . . ."

Selection of child

Liar
Child A mimes an activity, for example, writing. B asks "What are you doing?" A answers untruthfully, for example, "Playing football". B then has to mime playing football, and when asked what he is doing by C, B answers untruthfully, and so on round the circle.

Produce photos, drawings or masks showing the same face but each looking very different.

What is happening when you look at this face?
It's the same one but it looks different each time.
It is because something inside us changes.
What are these changes called?

Feelings.

So what do the faces show?

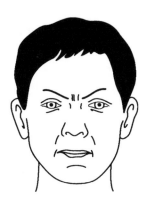

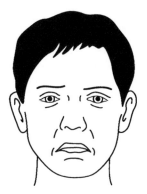

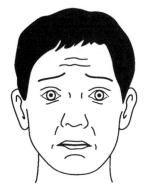

Being happy, sad, angry and frightened.

What are other words with the same meaning

"Have a look around, do you think anyone in this circle does not have feelings? Do you think I have feelings?"

It very much depends on the age and maturity of the children whether small groups are used at this point. If small groups are used, I would ask the children to find two others, perhaps with the same colour hair. Then they should take it in turns to tell the others "I can think of a time when I was happy. It was when . . . ." If it's been decided not to divide the children into small groups, ask for volunteers to begin. If there have been small groups, then give the opportunity for those that want to, to share with the large group at the end.

The teacher or leader can ask the children if it's all right and natural, for example, to feel angry. It's important to help the children realise that all kinds of feelings are acceptable. They are a very important part of everyone. They are not good, bad, right or wrong.

"Do robots have feelings? When we see them on television or in films it sometimes looks as if they have."

"Who can demonstrate what a really good stretch looks like? Now I would like everyone to stand, stretch as much as possible, and then crouch down. How do you feel as you crouch down? Then have one big jump, clap your hands above your head, and sit down again in the circle."

All hold hands and do a lighthouse. Remind children that the light from a lighthouse shines in order to help people. It shines in a friendly way helping everyone that is near it. Ask everyone to look around the circle, make eye contact with some, and smile. This should be a quick activity and done silently. It stops when the hands are parted, which the teacher initiates.

At the end of each Circle Time (if it's done at the beginning of the day) before anyone gets up, take the opportunity to announce what the plan for the rest of the day will be, to involve the children in the organisation, to remind them of equipment needed and where to find it, to tell them where they need to be at particular times, for example, appointments for doctors or swimming lessons. Point out the rules which have been jointly agreed and are on display so that everyone can have a happy and productive day. Do the children have any questions now? Any comments?

Circle Time to promote a sense of identity 2

A Sense of magic

Children love magic and mystery so it was with a sense of excited anticipation that the children entered their classroom on Monday morning. On the previous Friday afternoon each child had written their name on a small piece of paper, pushed the piece of paper into their own balloon and blown it up. The balloons were then suspended in a cluster from the ceiling.

I sat on the floor, shoes off, in a space that had been cleared of desks. As the children came in, I greeted each one by name and gestured to them to join me. Soon a circle was formed. I invited all the children to look round it, catch the eye of anyone they had not yet seen and to give that person a friendly wave or smile.

There was then a hush. What next? "What about making some noise?" My invitation was readily accepted. "Well then this is what we do." We stood, bent our knees and touched the floor with only the ends of our toes and the tips of our fingers. As we slowly unravelled and straightened up, our hum got louder and louder and when we were at full-stretch we jumped as high as we could and yelled as loudly as possible. We did this three times, making more noise each time - "So that the whole school can hear us!"

We sat down. We looked at each other. There was a comfortable feeling in the room. Circle Time had begun.

A round

"I'm . . . (name) and today I'm feeling . . . ."

Selection of child

Sculpting in threes

A is the sculptor; B is the model; C is the clay. A closes her eyes; B adopts a pose and stays in that pose. A has to feel B and then turn to C and put her in the same position. When all the As have finished they open their eyes and everyone decides how accurate the sculptors have been. Take turns to be sculptors, models or clay.

Group the children in pairs and give each pair a piece of blank paper. "Draw four columns on your piece of paper and head each column, happy, sad, angry and scared. Under each heading make a list of what things in this school give you these feelings. Think of all the things which happen to you from the time you arrive in the morning until you leave, not just in the classroom, but in the hall, corridor, toilets and playground. Then bring your lists back to the group where we will share them and see if they are similar or different."

This can lead to a large group discussion from which will undoubtedly emerge topics such as bullying. If necessary, these topics can be dealt with in further sessions.

All hold hands and do a lighthouse. Remind children that the light from a lighthouse shines in order to help people. It shines in a friendly way helping everyone that is near it. Ask everyone to look around the circle, make eye contact with some, and smile. This should be a quick activity and done silently. It stops when the hands are parted, which the teacher initiates.

At the end of each Circle Time (if it's done at the beginning of the day) before anyone gets up, take the opportunity to announce what the plan for the rest of the day will be, to involve the children in the organisation, to remind them of equipment needed and where to find it, to tell them where they need to be at particular times, for example, appointments for doctors or swimming lessons. Point out the rules which have been jointly agreed and are on display so that everyone can have a happy and productive day. Do the children have any questions now? Any comments?

Circle Time to promote a sense of identity 3

A Sense of Magic.

Children love magic and mystery so it was with a sense of excited anticipation that the children entered their classroom on Monday morning. On the previous Friday afternoon each child had written their name on a small piece of paper, pushed the piece of paper into their own balloon and blown it up. The balloons were then suspended in a cluster from the ceiling.

I sat on the floor, shoes off, in a space that had been cleared of desks. As the children came in, I greeted each one by name and gestured to them to join me. Soon a circle was formed. I invited all the children to look round it, catch the eye of anyone they had not yet seen and to give that person a friendly wave or smile.

There was then a hush. What next? "What about making some noise?" My invitation was readily accepted. "Well then this is what we do." We stood, bent our knees and touched the floor with only the ends of our toes and the tips of our fingers. As we slowly unravelled and straightened up, our hum got louder and louder and when we were at full-stretch we jumped as high as we could and yelled as loudly as possible. We did this three times, making more noise each time - "So that the whole school can hear us!"

We sat down. We looked at each other. There was a comfortable feeling in the room. Circle Time had begun.

A round

"If I were a famous person I would be . . ."

Selection of child

Train name game

The children stand and imagine they are passengers waiting at different railway stations. The teacher in the middle of the circle is the train warming up. After a few preliminary circlings she goes to a station to pick up the first passenger. She says "Good morning, what is your name?" The child answers, whereupon the teacher shouts the name five times, at the same time jumping and clapping hands. She then turns round and put her hands on the child's waist and they shuffle off to pick up the next passenger. The first child says "Good morning, what is your name?" The second child answers, whereupon the teacher and first child shout the second name five times and jump up and down. When the second child is collected, the train turns so the second child is in the front and has to ask for the name. Everyone on the train shouts the name of the new passenger and jumps up and down. As the train gets longer it can be split to make the game quicker!

The teacher mimes an emotion, for example, anger, by shouting, growling, flinging arms about, or joy, by smiling, laughing, jumping. Exaggerate all your movements and walk round the circle.

Ask for a volunteer (A) to come out and mimic you, and then ask if they can mime the opposite feeling. A then mimes a new emotion and chooses B to mimic him. Then B mimes the opposite feeling and so on. Continue while there are children willing to be chosen. No one should be coerced into miming.

or

This is an activity called For your eyes only. Grouped in triads, one child should take it in turns to look at the other two. No words, sounds, gestures, or movements of the face are allowed: all feelings are shown only in the eyes. The children being watched should allow themselves to feel the four feelings: happiness, sadness, anger, fear. Initially, the feelings should be done in a set order, for example, glad, sad, angry, scared. After everybody has tried it in this order then they can do it in any order to see if the observer can guess which emotions are being expressed.

 The above activity can conclude with a group feedback. Generate a discussion by using the following questions: "Was it hard to use only your eyes? Do you think that the eyes are a good place to look if you want to know how others are feeling? What other things do people do which show you how they are feeling, (for example, do you tap your feet when you're angry)?" Ask the children to demonstrate actions which express feelings.

Give the children a sheet of paper and ask them to fold it in four. Ask them to draw one face in each section demonstrating the emotions glad, sad, angry or scared. Then ask the children to list under their drawings as many words as they can, associated with each emotion. They can do this activity during the day or as a home task and then share their pictures and words the following day. Remind them that relatives and friends can help.

All hold hands and do a lighthouse. Remind children that the light from a lighthouse shines in order to help people. It shines in a friendly way helping everyone that is near it. Ask everyone to look around the circle, make eye contact with some, and smile. This should be a quick activity and done silently. It stops when the hands are parted, which the teacher initiates.

At the end of each Circle Time (if it's done at the beginning of the day) before anyone gets up, take the opportunity to announce what the plan for the rest of the day will be, to involve the children in the organisation, to remind them of equipment needed and where to find it, to tell them where they need to be at particular times, for example, appointments for doctors or swimming lessons. Point out the rules which have been jointly agreed and are on display so that everyone can have a happy and productive day. Do the children have any questions now? Any comments?

Circle Time to promote a sense of identity 4

A round

This round will be silent. Using the feelings pictures that were prepared in the previous Circle Time, each child, in turn, will hold up the picture which represents their present feeling. If they are feeling a different emotion and do not have a picture for it, their papers are kept down and their feelings are revealed at the end.

Selection of child

Getting into a tangle

Standing close together, everyone closes their eyes, and on a given signal stretches their arms out and finds a hand to hold. Then, opening their eyes, the children can see if it's possible to unravel the tangle they have created. It is sometimes easier to break into two groups for this activity especially if the group is large.

Begin by asking children to tell everyone the words they listed next to their feelings pictures. Collectively make a list of these words. Give out a vocabulary of feeling words sheet (page 65). The bigger vocabulary we have the better we can understand our feelings and express them to others.

"Now I would like you to find two others who you feel comfortable with. Sit cross-legged in a close triangle." Then ask them to label themselves A, B and C.

Ask C to choose five words from the feeling list. Then using these words brain-storm endings to the sentence stems in the following format:

> I feel bored when . . .
> I feel left out when . . .
> I feel loved . . .
> I feel silly when . . .
> I feel annoyed when . . .
> The children should take it in turns, picking five words each time from the list.

"Now I would like each group to prepare three very short plays or sketches. They can either be performed silently, in mime, or by use of words. This is how you do it. Each person picks a feeling word from the list and thinks of a situation where you have felt like that. Don't tell your group the word. Take it in turns to tell your partners where it was and what happened. Then act the situation in front of them. For example, you are at home in a room with your brother and sister. Your brother asks your sister if she would like one of his sweets. She takes one. He does not offer you one. You have to ask him for a sweet, and he then gives you one. How do you think you would feel?

"Another example could be: You and your friends are playing on your bicycles. You fall off your bike and hurt yourself. How do you feel? Act how you feel to the rest of your group. When you have all performed your plays in your groups we will get back into the large group and we will guess what each other's emotions are. Remember not to say the word and remember that feelings can usually be seen in the way people act, rather than from what they say." Use this opportunity to explain some rudimentary body language. About 60% of communication is non-verbal.

All hold hands and do a lighthouse. Remind children that the light from a lighthouse shines in order to help people. It shines in a friendly way helping everyone that is near it. Ask everyone to look around the circle, make eye contact with some, and smile. This should be a quick activity and done silently. It stops when the hands are parted, which the teacher initiates.

At the end of each Circle Time (if it's done at the beginning of the day) before anyone gets up, take the opportunity to announce what the plan for the rest of the day will be, to involve the children in the organisation, to remind them of equipment needed and where to find it, to tell them where they need to be at particular times, for example, appointments for doctors or swimming lessons. Point out the rules which have been jointly agreed and are on display so that everyone can have a happy and productive day. Do the children have any questions now? Any comments?

Display the vocabulary of feeling sheets in the classroom and refer to them when any appropriate situation occurs. Tune children into feelings whenever possible. Make masks representing the four feelings as a craft activity and use them in drama.

A vocabulary of feeling words

angry	excited	relaxed
annoyed	fearful	relieved
anxious	flustered	satisfied
apathetic	foolish	scared
bored	frustrated	serious
calm	glad	shocked
cautious	grieved	silly
comfortable	happy	solemn
confident	hesitant	stubborn
confused	hopeful	surprised
contented	jealous	tense
cross	kind	tired
daring	left out	trapped
despairing	lonely	troubled
discontented	loving	uncomfortable
eager	miserable	uneasy
elated	peaceful	warm
embarrassed	pleased	weepy
energetic	proud	wonderful

Can you think of any words to add to this list?

Write them here:-

Circle Time to promote a sense of identity 5

Opening Round
"I feel great when . . . ."

Selection of child

Locomotion
The child who is to have a Special Day can start this game by standing in the centre of the circle and performing any action, for example, waving, and at the same time indicates to three others in the centre of the circle who follow on behind imitating. The four children now indicate to others to join them. As the last one gets up and begins to do it, the others sit down, and the last one begins a new action and picks three others to mimic her, and so on. (Children like this opportunity to show the latest dance steps.)

"When I'm cross I . . . ."

"See if you can find two others with an initial the same as yours, or with the same number of letters in their name as you and sit down in a triad.

"Today we will have what I call a gripe time or an opportunity to complain. Take it in turns and complete the sentence: 'The things I don't like doing are . . . '."

After the triads have had time for a few gripes each, gather the group together for feedback. "What was it like having a gripe time? Who feels different now? Who can think of ways of dealing with strong feelings?" Generate discussion by asking the group some of the following questions: "We all know its good to laugh and smile. Is it all right for boys and men to cry? When is it all right to cry? What happens if you really want to cry but won't let yourself? What else can we do?"

During the discussion try to draw out from different children ways of coping with our emotions, for example, talking to someone, breathing quietly and deeply, writing our thoughts down, hitting things like cushions, even throwing newspaper balls.

Feelings that are suppressed don't go away and they manifest themselves in our behaviour. Children who are brought up having their feelings constantly denied will first learn to hide their feelings, then learn not to trust their feelings and may eventually learn not to feel. When children are out of touch with their feelings, or suppress their emotions, or are not aware of non-aggressive ways of expressing anger or frustration, conflict invariably surfaces.

"Repressed traumatic experiences in childhood are stored in the body and although remaining unconscious, exert their influence, even in adulthood."

Alice Miller: The Untouched Key, 1990

 Let everyone enjoy having a long stretch. This can be followed by a jump and shout if desired. Then sit down in the circle.

 "Everyone be really quiet, listen to your breathing, close your eyes gently and feel yourself relax from your head to your toes. All hold hands and do a lighthouse." Remind children that the light from a lighthouse shines in order to help people. It shines in a friendly way helping everyone that is near it. Ask everyone to look around the circle, make eye contact with some, and smile. This should be a quick activity and done silently. It stops when the hands are parted, which the teacher initiates.

 At the end of each Circle Time (if it's done at the beginning of the day) before anyone gets up, take the opportunity to announce what the plan for the rest of the day will be, to involve the children in the organisation, to remind them of equipment needed and where to find it, to tell them where they need to be at particular times, for example, appointments for doctors or swimming lessons. Point out the rules which have been jointly agreed and are on display so that everyone can have a happy and productive day. Do the children have any questions now? Any comments?

Drawn by a boy, aged 8, while experiencing the violent marital break-up of his parents.

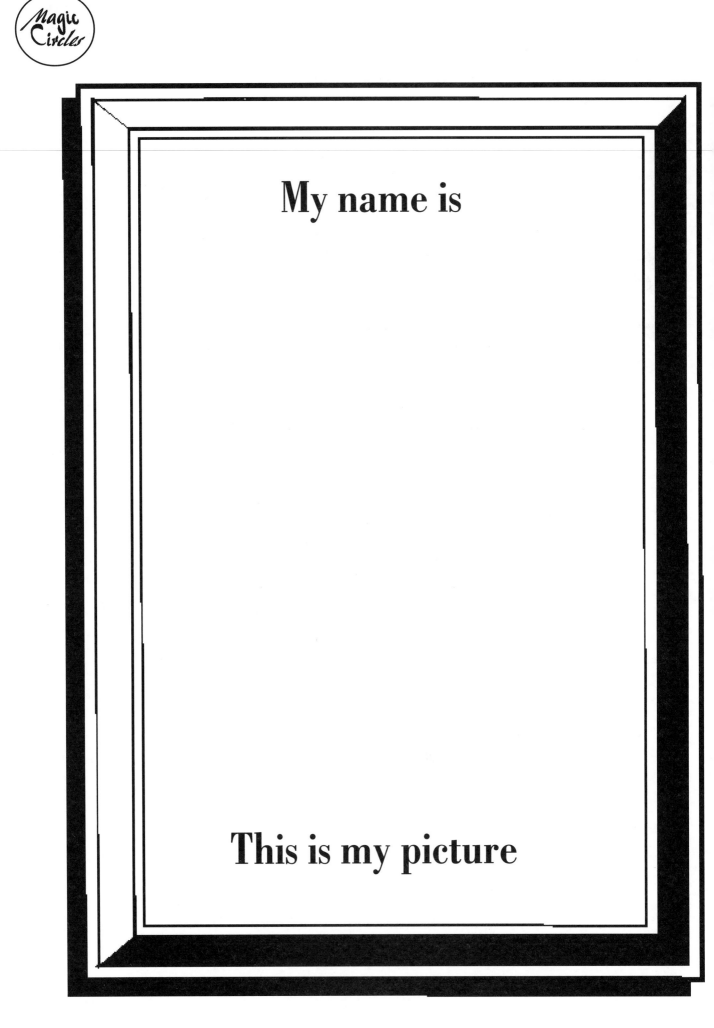

My name is

This is my picture

Circle Time to promote a sense of belonging

Circle Time to promote a sense of belonging 1

Opening Round

"The best thing anyone could do for me today would be . . . ."

Selection of child

Huggy bear

Children mill around and when a number is called must get into a group of that number and with their arms round each other's shoulders or waists sit in a circle. The last group to sit is out!

"Today I am going to ask you to find partners like this. Choose any number between one and ten and put that number of fingers up. Then see if you can find two others showing the same number. If you can't, go for the nearest number. Sit in a tight triangle, legs crossed. Name yourselves A, B, C.

"I want you to take one minute each to describe your partner using the sentence stem: "I see . . . ." A describes B and C is the observer. C counts the different things A says about B: "I see blue eyes, I see bitten nails, I see a smile, I see a tear in a pullover." See who makes the most descriptions." A small bell or quiet gong is useful to achieve good time keeping.

Bring the group together and ask the following questions to generate discussion. "What was it like describing your partner? When might it be important to describe someone well? Did you describe your partner well? Did he or she think so? Were you pleased with the description of yourself? What did it feel like when you were being described?"

Then ask a volunteer to describe someone in the room without looking at that person. After, the group will guess who is being described. It is helpful if the teacher demonstrates this.

Someone whispers a word or phrase into an ear of a neighbour who then passes it on. This continues round the circle until it returns to the originator who can tell the group if the word or phrase has altered. This is done most successfully by holding hands.

At the end of each Circle Time (if it's done at the beginning of the day) before anyone gets up, take the opportunity to announce what the plan for the rest of the day will be, to involve the children in the organisation, to remind them of equipment needed and where to find it, to tell them where they need to be at particular times, for example, appointments for doctors or swimming lessons. Point out the rules which have been jointly agreed and are on display so that everyone can have a happy and productive day. Do the children have any questions now? Any comments?

Circle Time to promote a sense of belonging 2

Opening Round

"I think a friend is someone who . . . ."

Selection of child

Group sculptures

Three volunteers go into the middle of the circle and are asked to form an interesting shape together (their bodies must be touching). The rest of the group (in triads) then make up their shapes. Afterwards the triads discuss the shapes they've made. Suggest that the triads try and make several different sculptures. Once everyone is regrouped in the circle, the triads can perform their shapes to the large group.

This activity should end with a whole group sculpture. The Special Day child can start the sculpture by going into the centre of the circle. He then names another child who joins to him in some way. This continues until the whole group, in a multitude of positions, is joined.

It is a good idea to take pictures of this activity. The display of such photos can help the growth of self-esteem.

Ask the children to look around the circle and count the number of children they have already spoken to today. Ask for examples of what they said to each other.

"Today I'm going to group you into triads by splitting up the circle like cutting a cake." Go round counting off threes. Make sure each group has a piece of paper and a pen or pencil.

"Find a good space for your triad and sit down please. I would like you to write down a list of things you would like to hear people say to you. For example, what would you like to hear from your classmates, your teachers or parents, your brothers and sisters, relatives and shopkeepers."

Bring the group back together and ask each triad to repeat their lists. Ask for volunteers to make up the lists into a well decorated book, which can then be displayed as a reminder.

Suggest that from today, and for the rest of the week, they should try and say the things to others that they themselves would like to hear. Next week ask if they did this, and if so, whether they noticed anything different?

Standing in a circle, holding hands, a coded message is sent round the circle by a number of short or long but always gentle squeezes. See if the originator receives the same message that he or she sent.

At the end of each Circle Time (if it's done at the beginning of the day) before anyone gets up, take the opportunity to announce what the plan for the rest of the day will be, to involve the children in the organisation, to remind them of equipment needed and where to find it, to tell them where they need to be at particular times, for example, appointments for doctors or swimming lessons. Point out the rules which have been jointly agreed and are on display so that everyone can have a happy and productive day. Do the children have any questions now? Any comments?

Circle Time to promote a sense of belonging 3

Opening Round

"A television advert I like is . . . because . . . ."

Selection of child

Categories

With the children sitting in a circle, the teacher calls out a category, for example, those whose name begins with A or those who have a pet. Children to whom this category applies should jump up and sit in the centre of the circle until the next category is called. The game should get faster and faster, ensuring that everyone is included.

The last category called should be Everyone in this room! When everyone is sitting inside the circle invite the children to have the biggest, longest silent stretch (like a cat) they have ever had, then to go back to their places.

"Earlier we thought of television adverts. What do all adverts set out to do? Sell things. Who can name a successful advert? How does it achieve its aim?

"Who can remember the first friend they ever made? Someone who was not related to you at all, so we won't count cousins, although of course they can be friends as well. Where did you meet this person? What happened? Can you remember who spoke first? Who asked the other to meet again?" Get the children to contribute their experiences. "Some people have lots of friends and some a few. Both groups are all right. I think most people think friends are important - think of the number of children here who get upset when they break friends. The funny thing is you will never know if someone is going to be a friend until you start talking to them. I always think of meeting a new person as an exciting adventure. It may be the person who is to become your very best friend in all your life. You'll never know unless you try.

"I want you to try something now. If I had the power I would now bring into the room a class of children who you didn't know at all - from another planet (not really) - but certainly from another school. I bet you that if I just said "All right, everyone get to know each other", you would very quickly do so. As we can't magic in strangers, we'll do the next best thing. I would like you to think of the children in this class who, for one reason or another, you have not talked to much." Pause for the children to consider. "Now, I'm going to ask you to get into groups with these children, and the way I want you to do it is this. Go up to one person and say

"Hello, shall we be in a group?" If you both agree, look round the room and decide between you which other pair you would like to join with, and then ask them.

 "When you are a four, sit down, closely together, and tell the others how you felt choosing a partner, and asking, or being asked. See if you can find out if there is a game which you all like very much.

"Now I would like you to make a television advert advertising a friend. Choose one person in the group who agrees to be advertised. Think how you can present them in the best possible way. Tell everyone all the good things this person does for others and why she would make a fabulous friend."

Suggest they make posters, and use music, props, and dressing-up clothes. Each group should present its advertisement to the large group.

 With hands crossed, swing from side to side, perhaps to music (as in "Auld lang syne").

 At the end of each Circle Time (if it's done at the beginning of the day) before anyone gets up, take the opportunity to announce what the plan for the rest of the day will be, to involve the children in the organisation, to remind them of equipment needed and where to find it, to tell them where they need to be at particular times, for example, appointments for doctors or swimming lessons. Point out the rules which have been jointly agreed and are on display so that everyone can have a happy and productive day. Do the children have any questions now? Any comments?

 An alternative to the television activity for young children could be a game, "Please Mr Policeman, have you seen my friend?" One of the children pretends he is lost and asks the policeman, "Please Mr Policemen, have you seen my friend?" The child then goes on to describe his friend to the policeman. For example, "He phones me if I'm ill", or "He helps me find lost things". Do not encourage descriptions of physical characteristics. The policeman guesses who is being described and if he cannot, then he can call in extra help to solve the case. Ensure everyone gets a chance to play all roles eventually.

Circle Time to promote a sense of belonging 4

Opening Round

Hold up a sign "Co-operation is . . . ."

"We are going to explore the meaning of the word co-operation today, and see what we can discover about it and what it means to us. As the sheet comes to you, hold it up to the group and finish the sentence."

Examples are:

Co-operation is to volunteer to do something in the group

Co-operation is to wait your turn

Co-operation is to be friendly

Co-operation is to listen

Co-operation is sharing with others.

Selection of child

Fruit salad

Give each child a name of a fruit - apple, banana, pear, orange, and repeat round the circle. Then call out one fruit and those who have the name of that fruit change places with each other. The last one seated is out. If you call fruit salad everyone moves. Let the children volunteer to do the calling.

Ask the children to mill around the room. When they are well-mixed ask them to close their eyes and gently find two others. Then ask the triads to prepare a playlet or sketch, which is a good example of children, or grown-ups, co-operating. Each triad should act their sketch to the large group.

"Join your triad to another triad. Now imagine one of you has a birthday coming and you are all going to the party. It can either be held at home or, for example, Macdonald's or the Happy Eater, or somewhere else. In your group, brainstorm all the reasons for and against where to hold it and decide which venue you would prefer. Each group then presents their reasons to the big group who will take a vote."

Tell the group they can have a party in school one day this week if they will arrange it themselves as a practical example of co-operation.

Shine a smile round the group.

At the end of each Circle Time (if it's done at the beginning of the day) before anyone gets up, take the opportunity to announce what the plan for the rest of the day will be, to involve the children in the organisation, to remind them of equipment needed and where to find it, to tell them where they need to be at particular times, for example, appointments for doctors or swimming lessons. Point out the rules which have been jointly agreed and are on display so that everyone can have a happy and productive day. Do the children have any questions now? Any comments?

Opening Round

"I was helped once when someone . . . ."

Selection of child

People machines

Ask for three volunteers and then ask if they can think of a way to pretend to be a washing machine. Show them how to hold hands with outstretched arms whilst the third pretends to tumble around inside as the laundry. Group the others into triads. Ask them to make a machine, for example, a car, typewriter or computer. Then each triad should demonstrate their inventions to the rest of the group.

Ask the children to find two partners who like the same desserts as they do, for example, yoghurt, rice pudding or apple tart. Give each triad two large sheets of paper.

"Now the other day we were thinking of things we like to hear people say to us. Today I would like us to spend time thinking about the opposite - the things we don't like to hear. Perhaps you have a name for statements like these. Any suggestions? Put-down is one, sarcasm or insult are others. They are really nasty and they hurt even though no one hits or punches. Make a list, now, of as many horrible things you don't want to hear as you can think of."

After a suitable time ask them to underline the three which they think are the worst, and then read them out to the big group. "Now, in your triads decide who will be A, B and C. Take one minute each and tell the others of a time, an experience, when you had a put-down from someone and how it felt. On the second sheet I gave you make a list of as many feelings as you can remember which you had when it happened."

Bring the groups back to the circle and ask the children which feelings they recorded. "I would like to ask you an important question. Would it be possible to create an environment in this room where there are no put-downs? How many would like to see this happen in here? Put up your hands if you would. In that case I suggest we have a ceremony to get rid of the put-downs."

Tear the put-downs listed on the first sheets into separate statements, then put them all into a prepared box - a shoe box or breakfast cereal box, coloured, or covered in black, and then if possible find somewhere convenient outside where the group can go to bury the box. Alternatively it can be burnt. Get children to arrange a ceremony they think appropriate.

All hold hands and do a lighthouse. Remind children that the light from a light-house shines in order to help people. It shines in a friendly way helping everyone that is near it. Ask everyone to look around the circle, make eye contact with some, and smile. This should be a quick activity and done silently. It stops when the hands are parted, which the teacher initiates.

At the end of each Circle Time (if it's done at the beginning of the day) before anyone gets up, take the opportunity to announce what the plan for the rest of the day will be, to involve the children in the organisation, to remind them of equipment needed and where to find it, to tell them where they need to be at particular times, for example, appointments for doctors or swimming lessons. Point out the rules which have been jointly agreed and are on display so that everyone can have a happy and productive day. Do the children have any questions now? Any comments?

No matter what you say or do to me I am still a worthwhile person.

"If someone forgets, and attempts to use any put-downs, I suggest you remind them by telling them something like this: "I feel that what you are saying is a put-down and I'd like to remind you that dead words have no life in this classroom." If you don't want to say all that, put two fingers in a V and make a noise like a snake, a hissing sound, to tell them that you recognise a put-down, and remember that no matter what anyone says or does they are still a worthwhile person.

The good things people can see in me are..

Circle Time to promote a sense of purpose

Circle Time to promote a sense of purpose 1

Opening Round

"Good morning everyone. If I have the chance today I would like to . . ."

Selection of child

The power game (1)

The aim of these simple games is to get across the message that goals can be achieved through determination and being prepared to learn to concentrate. It would depend on the ages of the children involved, but usually I delay any explanation until a discussion on goal setting takes place and treat it purely as a fun activity.

The adult demonstrates by standing and then saying, for example, "I will tap my left foot with my right thumb four times", and doing so. All the children are asked to stand and to copy. It is essential that everyone says the statement before the action. The use of the words "I will" is crucial.

Other examples are: "I will clap my hands six times." "I will pat my head with my left hand for eight counts."

The level of complication of instruction depends on the age of the children, as does the decision to count out loud.

Ask for volunteers to choose the activity. A helpful rule is not to allow activities which involve touching others. Tell the children that there are times when it is important to know what others are doing, and times when it is not. Make sure everyone is saying the "I will" statement and note the difference it makes.

Begin the discussion by asking the children which games they like to play, then elicit answers to the following questions. "Which of the games you have mentioned are played with other people? If it is a game involving more than one against one, what do you call members of a group playing against another group? Do you enjoy being a member of a team? What makes a good team? What does each member need to do to be a good team member? What are the ways each member can help the others?"

"Now, so that everyone gets more talking time I'm going to ask you to form triads. I would like you to choose two others who like playing the same games as you, any games from football and netball to board games like scrabble or snakes and ladders. When you have done so, sit together in a close triangle. Each triad needs a piece of paper and something to write with.

"Are you settled? Good. I would like you to imagine now that you have just been appointed the manager of a professional team. It doesn't matter what the game is, because the managers all have the same basic role - to look after the team and encourage it to win. They do this in a number of ways; they see how much the players are paid, they look after their health and try to keep them fit by employing doctors and others, they try to improve their skills by getting them to practice and using coaches to help them. Above all else they need to get players to believe in themselves that they are good players and have the ability to win. What would you say to the players before a game, at half time, at the end? Remember they have another game to play soon. For example she or he might say "Great work, keep it up" or "I saw you try really hard". Talk about and make a list of all the useful phrases you can think of which would encourage your players to be a good team."

After an appropriate time ask the children to return to the whole group and share their suggestions. Write these on a large sheet for display.

"When else is it good to make comments like this? Who else can they be said to?" Family and friends will be the most likely answers. Repeat the question and persist with it to see if someone will say "to yourself." If so, praise, pointing to appropriate phrases on the list. If not, tell the children that while it's really pleasant to hear other people saying things like these to you, the best person to say them is yourself. "Why is that? Other people who will do this may not always be around when you need them; sometimes people say these things and you don't always believe them. You are always there, and you should always be able to believe yourself.

"Pick a phrase from the list, the one you like best. Say it to yourself." Here modelling helps tremendously and the adult should pick a phrase and say it aloud. Ask for volunteers to share their favourite, get everyone to say theirs aloud at the same time.

"Everyone think of a time when you have had something hard to do, like learning new maths or spellings perhaps, or something you have not wanted to do, like cleaning up an untidy bedroom. Can you picture the scene? When you can, say your phrase, for example, "you can do it" and then see yourself succeeding, winning.

"This is called Self-talk. We all talk to ourselves all the time, although we often don't realise it. Does anyone know of things they say to themselves? It's very easy to say things to ourselves which are not helpful and do not encourage us. Things like "that was silly" or "you are an idiot". If you catch yourself saying them, say, "hey, that's not right, I'm OK.", or something similar. Remember if we want ourselves to win we must do the same.

"The list we've made consists of positive statements. We need to say them to ourselves all the time. If you think any negative thoughts change them to positive thoughts and you are much more likely to win at whatever you are doing.

"I'm going to give some time each day for people to share their experiences, to tell us what happens when they use positive thoughts to help them achieve something."

All hold hands and do a lighthouse. Remind children that the light from a light-house shines in order to help people. It shines in a friendly way helping everyone that is near it. Ask everyone to look around the circle, make eye contact with some, and smile. This should be a quick activity and done silently. It stops when the hands are parted, which the teacher initiates.

At the end of each Circle Time (if it's done at the beginning of the day) before anyone gets up, take the opportunity to announce what the plan for the rest of the day will be, to involve the children in the organisation, to remind them of equipment needed and where to find it, to tell them where they need to be at particular times, for example, appointments for doctors or swimming lessons. Point out the rules which have been jointly agreed and are on display so that everyone can have a happy and productive day. Do the children have any questions now? Any comments?

To be a winner say:

I'm sure you can handle it

Well done

I like the way you did that

Just take one step at a time

I have confidence in myself

You can do it

That's a good try

You'll get there

Try looking at it in a different way

Everyone makes mistakes and that's OK

Have another go

That's a really good, wonderful, lovely . . .

That's an excellent . . .

That's skilful, brilliant, fantastic, . . .

Circle Time to promote a sense of purpose 2

A sense of magic.

Children love magic and mystery so it was with a sense of excited anticipation that the children entered their classroom on Monday morning. On the previous Friday afternoon each child had written their name on a small piece of paper, pushed the piece of paper into their own balloon and blown it up. The balloons were then suspended in a cluster from the ceiling.

I sat on the floor, shoes off, in a space that had been cleared of desks. As the children came in, I greeted each one by name and gestured to them to join me. Soon a circle was formed. I invited all the children to look round it, catch the eye of anyone they had not yet seen and to give that person a friendly wave or smile.

There was then a hush. What next? "What about making some noise?" My invitation was readily accepted. "Well then this is what we do." We stood, bent our knees and touched the floor with only the ends of our toes and the tips of our fingers. As we slowly unravelled and straightened up, our hum got louder and louder and when we were at full-stretch we jumped as high as we could and yelled as loudly as possible. We did this three times, making more noise each time - "So that the whole school can hear us!"

We sat down. We looked at each other. There was a comfortable feeling in the room. Circle Time had begun.

A round
"If I could have things just as I want them . . ."

Selection of child

The power game (2)
This is a variation on Power Game (1). Three volunteers go to the centre of circle, silently decide on the activities they are going to do, and then on a given signal announce them, using an "I will" statement, and then execute them simultaneously. The aim is not to be distracted by what the other two are doing and complete the task without hesitation. Children who do so can be called "Winners".

The game can be made easier or harder by:
    a)   varying the number of children in the centre;
    b)   insisting the contestants stand facing each other;

c)   changing the number of activities to be performed, for example, "I will clap once, jump three times and hop twice".

Encourage those that have difficulty. End by having everyone doing it together.

"If you hear someone described as a winner what do you know about them? What do you have to do to be a winner? Can only adults be winners?

"Winners are those people who succeed in what they set out to do." Tell the group about the annual "Children of Courage" awards given to children who have overcome their handicaps, illnesses or accidents by bravery, determination and persistence. There may be children in the group with similar experiences or they may know someone else who has.

"Do you have to have a handicap etc. before you can become a winner?" Tell the children about Edison's determination to invent an electric light bulb, about Hillary's ascent of Everest, Bannister's attack on the four-minute mile and ask the children if they know of other examples.

Ask the children if they have read any fiction about children or adults who were winners, for example, Dahl's Danny Champion of the World, Forrest Wilson's Supergran.

"The game we played is called Power Game. Power drives things; we get power from wind, nuclear energy, coal etc. Where do people get their power from? We call it will-power."

Hold up a sign with "Will-power is . . ." on it. "Let's have a good think about will-power because it's very important for all of us. Let us try to describe it in other words so that we can get a really good idea of what it means."

The teacher starts by completing the phrase and then moving round the circle in turn, everyone completes the phrase in their own way. Passes should be allowed, but children who do should be invited to contribute at the end, as it is often the case that they only want more thinking time.

Examples are: Will-power is keeping going; will power is stickability; will-power is being determined; will-power is not giving up; will-power is feeling strong; will-power is being able to concentrate.

"Form triads now please. Today find two partners who have got the same size, or very nearly, hand span as yours." When the children are settled give them a choice in the way they tackle this activity.

"Please think of people you know or have heard about who you would call winners. They can be people in your family, perhaps a grandparent or cousin, or someone you have read about or seen on television who you would describe as a winner. Talk about them and what happened and then decide on one person you would like to tell the group about. You can do that in one of three ways. You can tell us about her, name who she was, what she did, where it happened, or draw a picture to show those things or mime what happened. I hope you will be able to agree on how to present it to the group. Any questions? You have ten minutes to prepare."

Return to the whole group and share the presentations. Remind the children about the value of positive statements. Ask them to guess which phrases these winners used.

An alternative, or additional activity, is to ask the children to make up a chart recording all the positive events in their lives. Reference to parents might be necessary for some of the information. The smallest success is worth recording; it might be very significant to the child. Every attempt, every risk at some new activity which succeeds is important to the person that does it. Children like the opportunity to present these artistically in a variety of ways.

Mary Brown

Date	Event	Date	Event
	born		rode a bicycle
	cut first tooth		won a prize at the fair
	said "dada"		got a swimming certificate
	walked		joined a judo club
	started nursery		slept in a tent

All hold hands and do a lighthouse. Remind children that the light from a lighthouse shines in order to help people. It shines in a friendly way helping everyone that is near it. Ask everyone to look around the circle, make eye contact with some, and smile. This should be a quick activity and done silently. It stops when the hands are parted, which the teacher initiates.

At the end of each Circle Time (if it's done at the beginning of the day) before anyone gets up, take the opportunity to announce what the plan for the rest of the day will be, to involve the children in the organisation, to remind them of equipment needed and where to find it, to tell them where they need to be at particular times, for example, appointments for doctors or swimming lessons. Point out the rules which have been jointly agreed and are on display so that everyone can have a happy and productive day. Do the children have any questions now? Any comments?

Each human being is born as something new, something that never existed before. He is born with what he needs to win at life. Each can be significant, thinking, aware and creatively productive in his own right - a "winner".

M. James and D. Jongward, Born to Win

Will-power is...

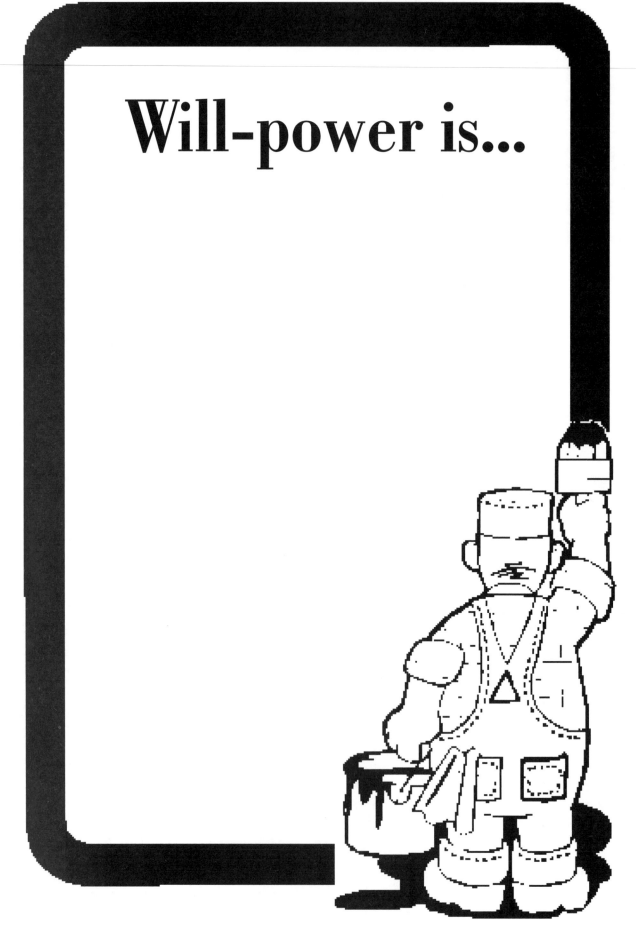

Circle Time to promote a sense of purpose 3

Opening Round

"I would like to help to . . ."

Selection of child

The power game (3)

Several volunteers go to the centre of the circle, make an "I will" statement and perform their activities all together, as in Power Game (2).

Now, however, time is introduced, test them to see if they can keep going for 30 seconds. After several turns this can be altered so the children do not know the time limit and have to wait for the adult's signal. They lose if they stop before time; those that keep going are winners.

Another variation is when a "fool" is introduced, a child who will dance around, make faces and try to distract the others.

"Do you know how to stretch? Winners know how to stretch. They aim for things which are just within their reach if they use their will-power. Just like teams use all their will-power to win their games, so do winners use all their strength to achieve their aims. Their aims are things they want to do, they go for a goal or a target.

"Today I would like you to think of some goals you would like to achieve, not big ones which you will do when you grow up, but small goals you can do today. Think of some things that you don't usually do that you would like to have done before bedtime tonight. Or perhaps something you would like to be better at doing or perhaps something you have never done and would like to try for the first time.

"Let's think of some examples. One might be where your teacher has often suggested that stories you write be longer. Today you can use your will-power to write half a page more than last time you wrote.

"Perhaps your locker is always untidy and you take a long time to find things. Today is the day when it will be put straight. Or would you like to be a neater writer? The way to tackle that big goal would be to choose just one letter that is not as good as it could be and really concentrate on improving it.

"It could be a physical skill you want to aim at - perhaps ten more skips than you usually do, five minutes longer at shooting at goal, seeing how fast you can become dribbling round skittles. The best sports people today started by setting small targets and going up one step at a time - some as far as the steps to the dais to get their Olympic medals.

"I would like you to think of some goals you can achieve outside school, for example, cleaning your teeth before you are asked to do it, helping to look after a younger brother or sister by playing a game with him or her, making your parents a cup of tea. What you choose should be something which would be good to do, and if you use your will power, possible for you to do.

"Find now please two partners who are exactly or very nearly the same height as you, and sit comfortably close together so you can easily hear each other talk. Everyone needs a paper and pencil. Decide who will be A, B and C. A will go first and tell B and C what her goals are - make a list of at least five. B and C are to share writing them down. When you have done that put them in number order, so you decide which one you will do first.

"B and C have turns at making a list of goals, then I want you to have your own sheets and write down next to each goal the name of anyone who you might want to help you in some way get that goal, to give you some advice perhaps or give you some equipment so that you can do it. It might be a friend, teacher, or relative. This person might also be the person you would like to tell when you have achieved your goal.

"Finally I would like you to write at the bottom of the sheet anything you think may stop you from winning. I could suggest that perhaps you will not give yourself time to do it properly, or you might forget. You might even decide you are too lazy to do it". Ask for examples. "This is called personal sabotage."

Bring the children back to the whole group. Ask if everyone understands. The aim is for everyone to do at least one task on their sheet today. Tell them "winners start today, don't delay". Remind them to give themselves some good self-talk.

 All hold hands and do a lighthouse. Remind children that the light from a lighthouse shines in order to help people. It shines in a friendly way helping everyone that is near it. Ask everyone to look around the circle, make eye contact with some, and smile. This should be a quick activity and done silently. It stops when the hands are parted, which the teacher initiates.

At the end of each Circle Time (if it's done at the beginning of the day) before anyone gets up, take the opportunity to announce what the plan for the rest of the day will be, to involve the children in the organisation, to remind them of equipment needed and where to find it, to tell them where they need to be at particular times, for example, appointments for doctors or swimming lessons. Point out the rules which have been jointly agreed and are on display so that everyone can have a happy and productive day. Do the children have any questions now? Any comments?

Circle Time to promote a sense of purpose (4)

Opening Round

"Something I wish I could have . . ."

Selection of child

The power game (4)

The aim of this activity is to demonstrate to the children how choices are made and the power of decision.

"In a moment I'm going to ask everyone to get up and go and do something. What that something is I'm going to leave completely up to you. The only rules are that it must be done inside the room, not hurt anybody or damage property. Just have a look around and think of all the possibilities there are open to you." (Only give examples if the children are very young.)

"I'm going to count to three and when I get to three I want you all to get up and do whatever you are going to do and then in one minute come back and sit in the circle."

Repeat several times. Observe those children who do this confidently without the need to copy others.

"Now I'm going to ask you to do it again. Have you decided what you will do this time? I shall count 1, 2, stop. See if you can change your mind quickly. Don't do what you were going to do, do something else instead as quickly as you can, now." Watch for children's reactions and how quickly they move.

"This is the last time. Ready? Have you decided what you would like to do? Now this one also has a little twist in it. When I count 3, I would like you to get up, go to wherever you were going and then decide not to do it and come back and sit down instead. Remember this is not me telling you not to do something, but you changing your mind and seeing how that feels. Ready, 1, 2, 3."

"I expect you have all heard the story of Alladin and his magic lamp. In the lamp was a genie who would come and grant any wish Alladin made. Have you seen the television programme Jim'll Fix It? Jimmy Saville is a bit like the genie. He makes wishes come true for people. Has anyone every had a wish come true?" Encourage children to share; self-disclose something of your own.

"Everyone has wishes and dreams. It is fine to have them. What we need to do is to see the difference between those that we can make happen and those we cannot. A boy told me once he hated the freckles on his face and so wished to get rid of them. No-one has ever thought of a way of doing that, even though science and medicine can do wonderful things. There are some things that is a waste of time and energy to wish for because they can never happen. It's more sensible to put all your effort into working to make those wishes that can happen actually come true.

Today I'm going to ask you to be by yourselves for a little while. Take a piece of paper and find somewhere quiet to sit on your own. On the paper draw a line down the middle and then on one side put down anything that you wish for which you know can never be, and on the other wishes that could come true. They can be wishes for today, or something which you would like to happen in the future, perhaps when you are grown up. You may draw pictures instead of using words if you wish."

After a set period tell the children how long they will have and let them know when there is two minutes left to finish. Bring them back to the whole group and ask them to share.

Be prepared for some personal disclosures and the feelings which accompany them. Stay with the wishes that can be accomplished. One wishes are expressed and recognised as normal, they are likely to motivate children into action. With emphasis on goal setting, children who have a history of failure and seem scripted for defeat, begin to realise that by the use of the will, some wishes may be attained. It becomes self-perpetuating and leads to more and more success.

Take one or two samples and by questioning the whole group put together a plan for the child to show how the wish can be attained. Make an action plan showing the small steps which will eventually lead to success.

Follow-up work is highly desirable, giving time and help to the child to see that she is getting enough support. Remind her to use her favourite positive statements, to write them down, and say them aloud and to share her aims with others.

If the opportunity can be given to help each child who has declared a realistic wish, the benefits will be both immediate and far reaching.

An alternative activity:
In triads, taking turns, A, B and C, and having three minutes each complete this round:
"If I had all the money I wanted the things I would do for myself would be . . . and for other people would be . . ."

In the whole group encourage free discussion. "Did your partners have some good ideas? Any you would do too? Were there any surprises? How important is money?"

All hold hands and do a lighthouse. Remind the children that the light from a lighthouse shines in order to help people. It shines in a friendly way helping everyone that is near it. Ask everyone to look around the circle, make eye contact with some, and smile. This should be a quick activity and done silently. It stops when the hands are parted, which the teacher initiates.

At the end of each Circle Time (if it's done at the beginning of the day) before anyone gets up, take the opportunity to announce what the plan for the rest of the day will be, to involve the children in the organisation, to remind them of equipment needed and where to find it, to tell them where they need to be at particular times, for example appointments for doctors or swimming lessons. Point out the rules which have been jointly agreed and are on display so that everyone can have a happy and productive day. Do the children have any questions now ? Ant comments?

For you to do

- Write down a short-term goal.
- What are the first concrete steps you could take to reach this goal?
- Action? Place? Time?
- Are you going to take these steps?
- What could keep you from reaching the goal e.g. - I don't want it badly enough, I'm afraid I might fail.
- What would it be like to succeed?

Circle Time to promote a sense of purpose (5)

Opening Round

I am looking forward to . . . or   I like to enjoy myself by . . .

Selection of child

The Power Game (5)

This is best played standing to allow for more variety of movement. The adult begins by making a sound and an action at the same time e.g. stamping on leg, waving and saying "hurray". As soon as the child on her left sees what it is, she copies, then the next child copies her and so on round the circle, each copying the person on the left, until everyone is doing it. After a few seconds the child on the left of the adult begins a new sound and movement which gets copied in a similar fashion. No-one ends one movement until she has a new one to copy from the left.

The children become very inventive with their sounds and movement. It gives them an opportunity in a very simple way to make a decision which affects others.

An enjoyable variation is when the group, through sound movement simulate a thunderstorm. The leader begins each movement which is then copied round the circle as before. It begins very quietly, reaches a crescendo, then gradually dies away. The sequence is: a) palms rubbed together, b) one finger tapping a palm, then two three, four fingers in turn, c) slow handclaps, d) loud handclaps, e) handclaps and foot tapping, f) fast claps and stamping, g) then reverse the order. Other stories in mime can be told in this way.

"We have been talking about goals and targets that each of you has set for your-selves. Today I would like us to think of a goal we can aim at all together. Like the game we have just played we shall all have to be in unison if we are to be success-ful.

What could we choose? What would give us all a good feeling if it was accom-plished by everyone. What is the burning issue in this group?" Ask for ideas, brain-storm, list them and do not comment - if a teacher says "good" about one idea and nothing about another, it not only influences children's opinions but inhibits fur-ther suggestions.

Discuss them, consider ways that all opinions can be respected and arrive at a truly democratic decision. The goal is more likely to be successful if chosen in this manner. Success in achieving one goal will lead to more being set and accomplished. Bring up the question of ways to help children who may find it difficult. Are there any practical solutions e.g. reminders from friends. Print out the difference between gentle encouragement and nagging - which do they prefer? Remind them of expressions that are used to help team members. Finally, tell them that each one of us is responsible for our own actions. We all need support, but as long as the goal is realistic and achievable then we will expect everyone else to do their bit and to win!

The goal should be measurable and specific, e.g., everyone to be punctual; everyone to have PE/games kit when required; only fuzzies and compliments to be used about others work or behaviour; a piece of work completed is set.

An additional or alternative activity:

"Choose two partners who have different colour eyes to you. Sit in a triad. On a piece of paper make a list of as many different activities which you can think of which you know other girls and boys have chosen to do but which you have never done." Examples are: learnt to juggle, grown flowers, made a den, stamp collecting.

After the required time return to the whole group. Make a list and leave on display. Children who have done any of the activities should be identified, perhaps listed if they are willing to help or advise anyone else who would like to try how to start.

Encouraging children to discover strengths like these in home, holiday, after school activities leads to more self-esteem and higher academic achievement.

All hold hands and do a lighthouse. Remind the children that the light from a lighthouse shines in order to help people. It shines in a friendly way helping everyone that is near it. Ask everyone to look around the circle, make eye contact with some, and smile. This should be a quick activity and done silently. It stops when the hands are parted, which the teacher initiates.

At the end of each Circle Time (if it's done at the beginning of the day) before anyone gets up, take the opportunity to announce what the plan for the rest of the day will be, to involve the children in the organisation, to remind them of equipment needed and where to find it, to tell them where they need to be at particular times, for example appointments for doctors or swimming lessons. Point out the rules which have been jointly agreed and are on display so that everyone can have a happy and productive day. Do the children have any questions now ? Ant comments?

This
Winner's Certificate
has been awarded to

for

Congratulations
Well done!
It is good to feel proud

Circle Time to promote a sense of competence

Circle Time to promote a sense of competence 1

 ### Children love Magic

Children love magic and mystery so it was with a sense of excited anticipation that the children entered their classroom on Monday morning. On the previous Friday afternoon each child had written their name on a small piece of paper, pushed the piece of paper into their own balloon and blown it up. The balloons were then suspended in a cluster from the ceiling.

I sat on the floor, shoes off, in a space that had been cleared of desks. As the children came in, I greeted each one by name and gestured to them to join me. Soon a circle was formed. I invited all the children to look round it, catch the eye of anyone they had not yet seen and to give that person a friendly wave or smile.

There was then a hush. What next? "What about making some noise?" My invitation was readily accepted. "Well then this is what we do." We stood, bent our knees and touched the floor with only the ends of our toes and the tips of our fingers. As we slowly unravelled and straightened up, our hum got louder and louder and when we were at full-stretch we jumped as high as we could and yelled as loudly as possible. We did this three times, making more noise each time - "So that the whole school can hear us!"

We sat down. We looked at each other. There was a comfortable feeling in the room. Circle Time had begun.

 ### A round

It was hard to do but finally I . . .

 ### Selection of child

 ### The Car Wash

Remind the children of the purpose of a car wash. The owner of the vehicle wants the vehicle to look at its best. The oil and petrol and servicing can be compared to the diet it needs, the car wash to make it clean and sparkling.

Ask the group to form two lines facing each other, close together. A volunteer stands at the top between the two lines facing the group. She puts the magic coin in the machine and enters the car wash, moving slowly and bending forward. As she goes through hands come from everywhere to stroke, rub, polish the head, shoulders, arms, legs and feet giving a real shine for the day.

Encourage gentle but firm strokes. Let all who wish to have a turn. This is a very popular activity. I strongly recommend that a car wash is offered to the Special Day child - it doesn't take a minute, although some other children usually manage to slip through as well - and is such a worthwhile experience. Many children (and adults) do not get the amount of touch they need for growth; this is a friendly, harmless way to give some. The car comes out smiling and ready to perform well!

An alternative more robust version, known as tunnels can be used where the lines stands almost touching. No arms or hands can be used and the volunteer, either upright or on hands and knees, has to push her way through the tunnel. I've witnessed some children who are usually very withdrawn welcome the opportunity to do this.

Ask the children what bragging and boasting means. is it like lying? Why do people do it? Refer to the adventures of Baron Munchausen Do they know anyone like that?

"I think it is important to know what bragging feel like, so I suggest we all have a turn. It is fine to do it when it's a fun activity like this. Let me give you an example: - I play the guitar. I am the best guitar player in the world. When I play everyone in the street outside stops to listen. I was not taught, but could play when I was very young, before I could walk etc., etc.". Really exaggerate so that children get the idea of how extreme it can be.

"Now I would like you to choose two partners who you think are good at telling stories and sit in a group with them. Choose A, B, C, so you know in which order you are going to speak. Bragging is not quite the same as lying. I would have been lying if I said I could play the guitar but couldn't. Bragging is about being able to play the guitar, and then claiming to be better than absolutely everyone else. Even the best football player in the world does not win all his matches.

Take turns and take about a minute each to tell your partners about something you do well, perhaps, a hobby you have or something you've learned at school, and boast about it for all you are worth."

After they have done that say "I would like you to try something else now. Have another round, talk about the same topic and tell your partners how good you are, something which makes you feel good doing, but without bragging. I want to encourage you to say things like "I do it well I am good at it, I know how to do it, I'm pleased with what I do. Don't be shy, this is not bragging. Your partners can help you if you dry up by saying " tell us more". They will want to know everything you do. Have more than one topic if you want to."

When each person finishes I would like the other two of you to say to her "thank you for telling us that", "it sounds as if you do it well", or something similar. It should sound the same to the person as having a nice pat on the back would feel,"

Return to the big group for summing up. Ask the children if they could see the difference between the first and second rounds. Did their feelings change? Were they uncomfortable bragging, or listening to others brag? What about the second round?"

Explain that bragging is usually caused by not feeling very sure about yourself so you try to make up for this by claiming to be better than others. People who do this need friends who will help them feel alright.

Emphasise that talking about ourselves and our ideas is important and is not bragging. When we can speak positively about ourselves, it helps us to learn, get on with other people and be happy.

Encourage the children to practice doing it during the day whenever they have an opportunity. Provide time for a check-up/feedback at the next session.

 All hold hands and do a lighthouse. Remind children that the light from a lighthouse shines in order to help people. It shines in a friendly way helping everyone that is near it. Ask everyone to look around the circle, make eye contact with some, and smile. This should be a quick activity and done silently. It stops when the hands are parted, which the teacher initiates.

 At the end of each Circle Time (if it's done at the beginning of the day) before anyone gets up, take the opportunity to announce what the plan for the rest of the day will be, to involve the children in the organisation, to remind them of equipment needed and where to find it, to tell them where they need to be at particular times, for example, appointments for doctors or swimming lessons. Point out the rules which have been jointly agreed and are on display so that everyone can have a happy and productive day. Do the children have any questions now? Any comments?

Circle Time to promote a sense of competence 2

Opening Round

"Good morning. I want you to know that I know how to . . ."

Selection of child

Name game

Each child is to think of something they consider themselves good at or a quality which they believe themselves to have or are developing - something which they are pleased to draw to the attention of the group. Give time for children to choose. Children who need a prompt can ask friends. The teacher can make suggestions. Then the round begins and the children prefix their name with the word chosen, for example, "I am mathematical John", "I am punctual Sarah". At the end of the round children can be invited to see if they can remember the description used by others.

These descriptions can be helpful when holding an appreciations circle. This can happen at any time, especially when it is not convenient to give a "special day" to one child, or at the beginning of a new term or the end of a year, or when the class has accomplished something by working together.

Each child in turn receives the compliments and appreciations of others in the group. The remarks should be as specific as possible, for example, "I liked it when . . ." and opinions prefaced by "I think . . . ", "I believe . . . ", etc. Adults can remind children that appreciations should be for what people are as well as what they do, for example, "I'm glad you are in this class", "I'm pleased to share this time with you".

If the opportunity can be given for these remarks to be written down so much the better. Sometimes children can be asked to circulate, writing their compliments on others' sheets of paper. The time given to this activity is well spent. Research shows that children who give compliments to others greatly increase their own self-esteem while doing so.

Now give out paper and ask the children to prepare for a television or radio interview. A reporter has got in touch to say that she is coming to interview them and in order to save time and so that they will have the opportunity to say what they want to say about themselves, she would like them to each prepare five questions which she can use when interviewing. Remind them that it is not bragging to speak positively about themselves. Help them to frame the questions. They can be about their best features, successes in the past - a piece of school work they are proud of

- something they liked finding out about, somewhere they've been, something they have done for others.

- ◆ What are you good at?
- ◆ What have you learnt to do recently?
- ◆ What would your best friend say about it?
- ◆ Name some good deeds you have done.
- ◆ What do you like to be called?
- ◆ When do you feel at your best?
- ◆ Talk about a hobby or game you like.

An alternative activity is to think of five compliments beginning with the words "I am . . ." and to get them to think of what they are rather than what they do. If a child says "I am a good footballer", ask him what qualities he has to have to be that - co-operative, quick thinking etc. Give lots of examples. The reason for the interview can be some special occasion in school or a more far-fetched one such as publicity for a proposed rocket trip.

When the questions are ready, choose to have the children sit in small groups or the big group, whichever is appropriate, and take turns to be interviewed by the others. Recording equipment adds realism.

Success diaries

This exercise can be used for the introduction of success diaries. Children who have the opportunity to record successes remember these when they are about to embark on another piece of learning, or new behaviour, and is a great morale-booster and confidence builder. The books can be a source of pride for years to come. They are good items to be able to produce when starting a new school, or to show to grandparents.

All hold hands and do a lighthouse. Remind children that the light from a light-house shines in order to help people. It shines in a friendly way helping everyone that is near it. Ask everyone to look around the circle, make eye contact with some, and smile. This should be a quick activity and done silently. It stops when the hands are parted, which the teacher initiates.

At the end of each Circle Time (if it's done at the beginning of the day) before anyone gets up, take the opportunity to announce what the plan for the rest of the day will be, to involve the children in the organisation, to remind them of equipment needed and where to find it, to tell them where they need to be at particular times, for example, appointments for doctors or swimming lessons. Point out the rules which have been jointly agreed and are on display so that everyone can have a happy and productive day. Do the children have any questions now? Any comments?

Circle Time to promote a sense of competence 3

Opening Round

"This week I am especially interested in . . ."

Selection of child

Decisions

"Today I am going to ask you to make lots of decisions. To start there is a choice of activity. You can either choose to have a noisy time by having a jump and a yell, or a quieter time by sitting upright and concentrating on your breathing with your eyes closed. Those people who want to do the first show your hands; the second activity show yours. Now get into position where you will disturb no-one else, and then you have one minute to do what you have chosen before returning to the circle.

"The next thing I would like you to do is to choose two partners and find a space to sit in." When they are ready to proceed say "I have asked you to make people machines before. Today I am going to ask you to do this again with a slight difference. I want you to choose to make a machine which you think is one of the top ten most useful machines in the world. When you have picked one use your bodies to show it working in some way and when you have practised it to your satisfaction find another triad to demonstrate it to. If those boys and girls can guess what it is, give yourselves a pat on the back. Start when you are ready. You have 15 minutes to do everything before I shall ask you to return to the circle."

Give no more instruction than this, and no reminder about time. Be sensitive to the needs of children when forming the triads but hold back from making suggestions or giving help unless absolutely necessary.

"So what was that like? What a lot of decisions I asked you to make. First, finding partners, did you do the asking or did you wait to be asked? Who decided which machine you would make? How many suggestions did you have to choose from? How did you choose which other triad to ask to see your machine?"

Allow time for children to respond to the questions, and be ready to encourage any who may feel anxious about contributing.

"How many decisions have you made already today? What were they? For example, when to get up, what to eat, wear, which way to come to school, who to talk to when you got here. Do you think you can live without making decisions? Only if you let other people make them for you. Would you want that? It would mean other people telling you what to do all the time - which books to read, which programmes to watch, which football team to support, which toys to play with.

"The older you get the more decisions you can make for yourself so that you get a choice to live your life as you want it. Being able to think things through and make wise decisions is a big asset to everyone. Can anyone give an example of someone they know making a decision that really helped them? What decisions have your parents made which affected you, for example, moving house, going on holiday?

"I would like you to return to your original groups of six now and discuss this issue. Imagine that you all have a birthday in the near future and your parents have offered you the choice of celebrating it by having a party in your own home or taking some friends out for a meal, perhaps to Macdonald's or Pizza Hut. Everyone put forward their reasons for and against for both places. Then all have a turn at saying what her choice would be and why."

Return to the whole group and ask for contributions. "Was it an easy or hard decision? Did others think of reasons you had not thought of? Were you influenced by the decisions of others?" Emphasise the value of examining all the options before arriving at a decision.

An alternative or additional activity would be to ask the children in groups of six to consider the games which are played in Circle Time and to choose the ones they like best, giving reasons. They could go on to discover the ingredients of a good game, for example, pleasure and enjoyment, fairness, co-operation and clear rules. It is like making a cake, each part is important, they have to be mixed properly for something good to be made. Between them can they invent a game which they can demonstrate and then get the whole group to play?

All hold hands and do a lighthouse. Remind children that the light from a light-house shines in order to help people. It shines in a friendly way helping everyone that is near it. Ask everyone to look around the circle, make eye contact with some, and smile. This should be a quick activity and done silently. It stops when the hands are parted, which the teacher initiates.

At the end of each Circle Time (if it's done at the beginning of the day) before anyone gets up, take the opportunity to announce what the plan for the rest of the day will be, to involve the children in the organisation, to remind them of equipment needed and where to find it, to tell where they need to be at particular times, for example, appointments for doctor or swimming lessons. Point out the rules which have been jointly agreed and on display so that everyone can have a happy and productive day. Do the children have any questions now? Any comments?

Circle Time to promote a sense of competence 4

Opening Round

"Something I have done well recently is . . ."

Selection of child

Instructions

Demonstrate, by asking the children to give you detailed instructions, how to water a plant. Have all equipment ready. Obey their instructions literally or without thinking, for example, if asked to get water - get it in your hand, or take a jug and hold it by the spout. The children will soon get the hang of it. Ask them to perform other simple tasks, and to learn how important it is to be precise.

Alternative game

Mime something good. Ask the children to mime something they enjoy doing or can do well.

Begin by telling the children a story, if possible of a particular incident personal to yourself. Tell the story twice. In the first version blame everything that happens to you on anyone and everything around you. In the second one own responsibility for everything that happens. An example would be an elaboration of a story about a minor traffic incident:

"I was driving to school at the correct speed and making sure I was aware of all the other vehicles and pedestrians in the road. As I approached a junction I saw some children making a nuisance of themselves on the pavement then, without warning, a car came out of a side road and hit me. It was completely his fault."
and
"I was in a hurry to get to school as I was late getting up and still feeling tired. There were some children on the pavement waving to some others so my attention was distracted and I did not see the car coming out of the side road in front of me, so we collided. I was not able to stop in time."

Ask the children to identify the differences. Ask who it is that really gets harmed when we choose to ignore taking the responsibility. Is there ever a valid reason for not telling a story accurately?

Either in small groups or the whole group, encourage the children to share experiences of this kind, if possible, giving two accounts of the same incident in the way described.

Tell them that it is often easier to blame others than it is to take responsibility ourselves when something is not right. Point out that it is always possible to change our own actions, but not necessarily those of others.

Reports

Get the children to make some kind of self-assessment frequently. Ask them who is ultimately responsible for their learning? What is the teacher's function?

An opportunity to record their comments in a book devoted to the purpose, suitably embellished with their own artwork might be welcomed. If this is agreed with the children, parents can learn a lot about the children from them.

Examples:

This week/year I am pleased with the way I have . . .
I have enjoyed . . .
I have not enjoyed . . .
Next week/year I shall . . . differently.

All hold hands and do a lighthouse. Remind children that the light from a lighthouse shines in order to help people. It shines in a friendly way helping everyone that is near it. Ask everyone to look around the circle, make eye contact with some, and smile. This should be a quick activity and done silently. It stops when the hands are parted, which the teacher initiates.

At the end of each Circle Time (if it's done at the beginning of the day) before anyone gets up, take the opportunity to announce what the plan for the rest of the day will be, to involve the children in the organisation, to remind them of equipment needed and where to find it, to tell them where they need to be at particular times, for example, appointments for doctors or swimming lessons. Point out the rules which have been jointly agreed and are on display so that everyone can have a happy and productive day. Do the children have any questions now? Any comments?

Circle Time to promote a sense of competence 5

Circle whisper

Start the day by holding hands and sending a positive message round the circle. The leader whispers the message into the ear of the child on the right or left, who passes it on to the next person in a similar fashion, and so on until the person who sent the message receives it herself. "Have a good day", "Be happy", "Try something new today", are examples. Let the children initiate the message. Remind them that it should be something they want to hear themselves.

A round

"I'm . . . (name) and I am proud that I . . ."

Back writing

In pairs ask the children to use their fingers to write a word or phrase on their partner's back. Demonstrate first. Ask them to make only positive statements, for example, "to the top", "go for it", "I like you". The recipients can either say what the words are or have paper and pencil ready to write them down and then ask their partners to confirm if they are correct.

Variations include writing on the palm of the hand or forehead with the recipient's eyes closed.

"Choose two partners who are making the funniest face and sit closely together so you can talk. Decide in which order you will speak. Tell each other about either the funniest time or the most enjoyable time you can remember."

In the whole group ask them to recall any of their partner's funny experiences (with permission of course). "What makes people laugh or smile? What different kinds of laughter are there? Who will demonstrate? Are there any volunteers to try to make us laugh? You can tell a joke, clown about or just by laughing see if you can get us to join in."

At the end ask if smiling and laughing helps people to do their work better and to get on well with others. Is it a useful characteristic to be able to get people to laugh and smile.

"Knock, knock."	**"Who's there?"**
"Doctor."	**"Doctor Who?"**

Circle wave

Each child has a turn to give a wave to someone else in the circle. Then everyone waves together - as if they have just seen a friend they have not seen for a long time, perhaps at the airport reception area. This can all be done silently or when everyone is waving saying "hello" and "how are you?" can be allowed to get to a really friendly crescendo!

Rounds

"Today/this week/this weekend/this holiday I am looking forward to . . ."

"Today/this week/this weekend/this holiday I wish everyone . . ."

 All hold hands and do a lighthouse. Remind children that the light from a lighthouse shines in order to help people. It shines in a friendly way helping everyone that is near it. Ask everyone to look around the circle, make eye contact with some, and smile. This should be a quick activity and done silently. It stops when the hands are parted, which the teacher initiates.

 At the end of each Circle Time (if it's done at the beginning of the day) before anyone gets up, take the opportunity to announce what the plan for the rest of the day will be, to involve the children in the organisation, to remind them of equipment needed and where to find it, to tell them where they need to be at particular times, for example, appointments for doctors or swimming lessons. Point out the rules which have been jointly agreed and are on display so that everyone can have a happy and productive day. Do the children have any questions now? Any comments?

Circle Time to promote a sense of well-being

Circle Time to promote a sense of well-being

The activities following are designed to alleviate stress and promote a sense of well-being. They may be used in any Circle Time - use them frequently.

A new icon apprars in this section to indicate a visualisation or relaxation activity

Moan time
"I get upset by . . ."
"I hate it when . . ."

Use these rounds to give the opportunity for children to say what is troubling them, whether it is caused by anger, fear, frustration, or disappointment. Encouraging the expression of these feelings is healthy; children learn that everyone has them and that they don't have to be ashamed of them or repress them. We first have to recognise what's happening inside, then we can deal with it.

If any difficulties that are aired can be resolved in the group so much the better, but that is not the prime purpose of the activity, which is to acknowledge feelings. Generally "why" and "when" questions are not helpful, it is far better to support the speaker with remarks such as "it sounds as if that's really unpleasant/worrying/ annoying to you", and leave it at that.

Circle squeeze
Ask how we can give strength to others. Often we touch them and have feelings of support for them.

"All join hands and close eyes. Gently but firmly take the hands of those on either side of you. Imagine that everyone in the circle needs your help and support. Sit quietly for a moment and through your hands send your help and support to everyone (pause). Now think of everyone sending their support to you. See if you can find a good feeling inside which comes from being here with everyone else."

Deep breathing
"Sit upright or kneel and put your hands, palm downwards, on your stomach so that the tips of the fingers are just touching each other. Begin to breathe slowly and deeply, in and out and as you do so, feel your fingers separating and coming together. Close your eyes, maintain a steady rhythm and enjoy the peaceful feeling that comes with it."

Listening

Repeat breathing exercise, then invite children to sit or lay quietly and comfortably on the floor.

"This activity is about listening, really using your ears. You will find you can do this better if you close your eyes. First I would like you to see if you can identify any sounds you can hear that are coming from outside the building. Can you hear people or vehicles or machines or animals or birds? Listen to them for a moment (pause).

"Now can you hear any sounds or noises being made inside the building - telephones, people moving about, doors opening or closing? Listen to them (pause).

"Now listen to sounds being made in this room. Can you hear anyone moving or breathing. Anything apart from my voice? (pause).

"Last I would like you to try to cut out all the other sounds and spend a short time just listening to the sounds inside yourself - the quiet, steady breathing we can all do. Just enjoy listening to your breathing (pause).

"When you are ready I would like you to open your eyes, sit up, have a good stretch, look around the room, and then come back into the circle."

Discuss how we can choose what to hear, and how much we can miss because of the way we are. Ask the children if and when they experience silence and what their feelings are about it. Mention different life-style options - in the city, in the country, living in a crowd, living alone. We all have a choice.

The quick relax

Step one: "Be aware if you are upset (for example have a pain, headache, sweaty palms, fast heart beat etc.)."

Step two: "Smile inwardly and tell yourself to become calm."

Step three: "Now I would like you to imagine that the surface of your feet is covered with tiny, magic holes." (The children may giggle at this but the image appeals to them.) "They are usually covered by shutters but you can open them with your mind at any time.

"Do that now and then, breathing slowly and easily, think of cool air flowing through the holes, up through your legs into your stomach. Hold the air like that for a second and then let it go back down your body and legs, out through the holes, taking all your tensions and worries with it. Do that several times at your own speed.

Step four: "Go in your mind to that place where you are fully relaxed and happy - wherever that particular place is - perhaps a bed, someone's lap, playing with a pet, on a bicycle. Imagine all the details:

What are you wearing? Who is with you?

What can you hear, smell, touch?

What are you feeling inside now?"

Ask children to think of times in the past when it would have been helpful to know how to relax quickly. Is it a useful thing to do on occasions? Where in their bodies do they feel the tension? (Each of us usually has a favourite place!) Remind them of the power of self-talk and the phrase "no matter what you say or do to me I am still a worthwhile person". Some children enjoy doing longer relaxation exercises and being introduced to yoga.

Going on a trip

Ask the children to find a space and to either sit upright or lay down on their backs.

"Today we are going to use our imaginations, that part of the mind that sees pictures and can create anything we wish. Before we start, slowly and quietly take some deep breaths. Inhale, hold the breath for a moment, then slowly release it. Feel your body becoming relaxed and comfortable, the floor supporting you. And as your body becomes still, your mind becomes open and alert.

"Now I would ask you to let your imagination take you to a small island. It's got fields, trees, streams, a river, a beach, and the sea. It's a lovely place, somewhere you like to be. The sun is shining and warm, the wind is blowing gently, the birds are singing. You can decide just where you want to go, do what you want to do. Think of one thing you would like to do, walk in the woods, climb to the top of a tree, sit in a field, lie on the beach, paddle in the sea. You decide and then do it (pause).

"Really enjoy doing it. Feel the grass or the sand or the water, whatever it is. Do what you like without hurrying, no-one is going to tell you to do something different. Is there anything to hear where you are? . . . anything to smell? . . . anything to touch? What is the best thing about being where you are - on your island? This is a special place you have found. Really enjoy being there and how wonderful it is (pause).

"Remember this is a place you can return to at any time. Now, in your own time, when you are ready, I would like you to come back to the classroom. Have a slow stretch, open your eyes, sit up and then return to the circle."

Discovering our inner strength

"I would like you to find a space and get as comfortable as you can. So that you can really relax and enjoy this, take some deep breaths, very quietly so no-one else can hear. Draw the breath in, hold it and then slowly release it. Do this several times. Check your body, your arms and legs, everywhere, to see if you can feel any tension. If you can, send some relaxing breath to that place. When you are ready, close your eyes and start to enjoy the feeling of going on a journey in your imagination.

"It starts with you in a field. The grass is just as you like it, there are some flowers growing in it and perhaps some little creatures scurrying around going about their business. You are enjoying being there, the sun is shining and everything is fine. You can see a path which leads into some woods so you decide to walk along it. You cross the field and walk into the woods, perhaps kicking up the leaves as you go or looking out for rabbits or squirrels. As you go further you realise that the wood is at the bottom of a mountain. You decide to climb it and you are soon on an open path going upwards. It gets quite steep, but that doesn't stop you. You have plenty of energy and now you are determined to reach the top. There are easy parts, there are rocky places. Your legs are working hard, you breathe deeply and feel strong. You go on and on, up and up, until finally at last you are there. You find that it is a really beautiful place and you are pleased to have reached it . . . (pause).

"Sitting there already you see a child who waves and smiles at you. You both move to meet and greet each other. Soon you are talking and playing together as if you have been friends for a long time. You know that this person is special to you and will always be your friend. You know you can talk about anything with your friend and you will always get help and support and good company. If there are any questions you want to ask, you will always get a good answer . . . (pause). You can always trust this person to know what is best for you . . . (pause). You really enjoy being with your friend and doing the things you both like doing. You have more fun than you've ever had . . . (pause).

"Now it's time to leave. Your friend says you can come back at any time and you say you will visit often. You say good-bye and go back down the path and through the woods feeling very pleased to have met your friend and to know you can return whenever you want.

"The path leads you through the field and comes to the school gate. You walk through and into the school and into this room. Have a stretch and yawn. Open your eyes gently and when you are ready come back into the circle."

Then allow the children time to draw or write about their experience. The paper and materials should have been given out before the visualisation so that they can begin immediately without interruption. Follow up with a discussion with volunteers showing their drawings and talking about them. If time is limited have the discussion only.

To the top
name

When I get to the top I will have

Bibliography

Assagioli, R. (1984) The act of will. Turnstone Press.

Axline, V. (1971) Dibs, In search of self. Pelican.

Dewey, J. (1963) Experience and education, Collier Macmillan.

Douglas, T. (1983) Groups. Tavistock   Press.

Ferruci, P. (1988) What we may be. Turnstone Press.

Glasser, W. (1925) Control theory in the classroom. Harper Low.

Miller, A. (1990) The untouched key. Virago Press.

By the author.

White, M. (1995) Raising Self-esteem: 50 Activities. Folens.

White, M. (1995) Encyclopedia of social interventions. Chapter, Magic circles to enhance self esteem. Institute of Social Interventions. London.

White, M. (1993) Chapter 6, Developing self esteem in schools, in Counselling in Schools. Ed. Bovair, K. and McLaughin, C. Fulton.

White, M. (1995) Mentors, Masters and Mrs Macgregor, in Health Communications. Florida.

White, M. (1999) Picture this. Guided Imagery for Circle Time. Tape and booklet from Lucky Duck Publishing.

Esteem Workshops

Workshops for Professionals
for teachers, ancillaries, heads, advisors, governors and everyone involved in education.
- The Nuts and Bolts of Self-Esteem - strategies to promote a positive climate in school.
- Children Causing Concern - understanding behaviour and ways to help children cope with problems.
- Magic Circles - an introduction to the philosophy of Circle Time, with a 40-minute video showing it in action.
- On a Good Day I Can Teach for Ever - teachers' professional development.
- Building Staff Self-Esteem - whole staff development, ways to boost morale and increase co-operation.
- Counselling for Professionals - supporting teachers teaching.
- Appraisal - essential techniques for appraisers and appraised.

Workshops for the Public

♦ How to Raise Your Self-Esteem - strategies for personal development.
♦ Inter-Personal Skills - how to relate to others, at home and at work.
♦ Using visualisation to make life choices.
♦ Assertion - how to use it without fear or guilt.
♦ Job satisfaction and success in life.
♦ Listening is more than hearing - valuable listening techniques.

Workshops for Parents

♦ Parent Link - relating to your children. Weekly or weekend groups (in association with Parent Network, London).
♦ How to Help Your Child Cope with Stress.
♦ How to Raise Your Child's Self-Esteem.

Workshops for Children and Teenagers

♦ Celebration - an introduction to Circle Time, with parachute games.
♦ Social Skills Groups - small numbers for intensive personal development.
♦ Personal Development for Teenagers.
♦ Individual sessions to enhance self-esteem.

Also offered:

♦ Individual counselling and therapy, both crisis and developmental. Ongoing support groups for teachers and others.

The Circle Time Network

If you have Circle Times in your classroom, or are considering doing so, and would like contact with others that do, please write to the author. Circle Times are now happening in schools countrywide. Everyone involved is finding an exchange of ideas and experience about the benefits of Circle Times is valuable.

The International Council for Self-Esteem

- is a world-wide organisation that is created to promote public and personal awareness of the benefits of a healthy sense of self-esteem and responsibility.

Murray White represents this country on the International Council. For details of conferences and its other activities contact this address:

Esteem Workshops,
5 Ferry Path,
Cambridge, CB4 1HD.
Tel & Fax: 01223 365351
e-mail esteemhere@aol.com